Kevin's Glossary

ASTRONOMY

Kevin Ash

ABD PUBLISHERS
Jaipur ■ New Delhi

ABD PUBLISHERS

Regd. Off. "Bony Residency", Gate No. 2
Opp. Tilak Public School, Vishweswariya Nagar,
Gopalpura Road, Jaipur - 302018, India
Ph: 0141 - 2761280, Telefax: 2761381
Email: abdpublishersjpr@gmail.com

Delhi Office: 102, 1st Floor, Satyam House,
4327/3, Ansari Road, Darya Ganj,
New Delhi - 110002, India
Ph: 011-45652440

visit us: www.oxfordbookcompany.com

Published in India, 2024

ISBN : 9788185771723

Price : ₹ 1500/-

Typeset by Shivangi Computer, Jaipur

Printed and bound in India by Thomson Press Ltd.,
New Delhi

Preface

The reader's choice between these complimentary books will depend on his or her needs and preferences. The present glossaries are straightforward manual and compilation of terms relating to different subjects like, **Computer Science, Zoology, Botany, Physics, Chemistry and Astronomy** for accessing the depth of the subject. I have made it a point that the authors endeavour to gather almost all the terms which are required to understand the subject but I admit this series of Glossaries is by no means a definitive source for all the terms. I am only just beginning to present supplementary but fundamental books which have gathered and compiled various terms from different sources. You will notice that there may be more than one ways of expressing of the meanings of any term and as far as possible we have used them have. These Glossaries will be useful for an individual new to the subject or anyone inexperienced in dealing with some aspects of the subject. I would like to thank many people for their encouragement and assistance in the production of these Glossaries. I especially thank Prof. Brian James, I wish to thank Dr. Michael Genes of the University of Carrera for many comments that helped me improve the text of Glossaries and Mrs. Maria Charles - Swami, Reference Librarian at the University of Carrera, who was an enormous help in my efforts to use the university's electronic library. Many reviewers greatly helped improve the quality of this edition. I specifically wish to thank all of them.

Lastly, thanks are due to the many teachers and students, particularly those who have helped clarify points, find errors, and discover new and interesting ways of looking at the many topics collectively in the form of glossaries.

Kevin Ash

Kevin's Glossary

ASTRONOMY

16-Bit Systems : Such systems work with information in 16-bit chunks (words), i.e. they process two bytes at a time. In theory, 16-bit processors can operate faster and address more internal memory than 8-bit systems (typically 256 K instead of 64 K). In practice, what happens depends to a great extent on the operating software. Bigger and more modern systems work with 32-bit words, or even larger ones.

21 Centimeter Emission : A radio wavelength emission that originates with a neutral hydrogen atom, i.e., a single proton, or hydrogen nucleus, with its accompanying electron. The proton and the electron each have a quantum "spin", which points either "up" or "down." They can both be "up" or "down" (Parallel spins), or one can be "up" and the other "down" (antiparallel spins). The antiparallel state has slightly less energy than the parallel state, so if an atom in the parallel state changes to antiparallel, a 21 cm radio photon is emitted. Thus, cold neutral hydrogen in space emits this radiation which can be detected using a radio telescope. A direct, circular, low inclination orbit in which the satellite's orbital velocity is matched to the rotational velocity of the planet; a spacecraft appears to hang motionless above one position of the planet's surface.

8-Bit Systems : These deal with information in eight-bit chunks – or words – i.e. they process or transfer one byte at a time (see also 16-bit systems).

A

A index : A daily index of geomagnetic activity derived as the average of The eight 3-hourly a indices. A pattern of small cells seen on the surface of the Sun caused by the convective motions of the hot solar gas. A protocol used in an attempt to eliminate inhibitors once they are formed. It involves giving daily infusions of high amounts of a specific factor to reduce the immune system's response to factor so that the body does not create antibodies to factor. A region of charged particles in a planet's upper atmosphere; the part of the Earth's atmosphere beginning at an altitude of about 25 miles and extending outward 250 miles or more. A Renaissance Catholic court instituted to seek out and prosecute heretics.

A programme to help the user create, edit and update files of information.

Aangular momentum : Any object spinning or orbiting about a point carries angular momentum. This is basically related to the size and mass of the object. As spinning objects contract, they must spin faster to conserve angular momentum, or else fragment in order to share the momentum among the different parts. This is significant in astronomy in causing stars forming out of slowly rotating clouds to form as pairs or multiples or to form planets as the Sun did. In the Solar system, while the Sun contains 1000 times as much mass as all the planets combined, the planets account for 99.7% of the angular momentum. It is believed that the rapid spin rates of neutron stars are a result of the need to conserve angular momentum.

Abbreviated Dialling : The facility to code telephone numbers so the user can call them by pressing just a couple of keys.

Absolute Brightness (Absolute Magnitude) **:** A measure of the true brightness of an object. The absolute brightness or magnitude of an object is the apparent brightness or magnitude it would have if it were located exactly 32.6 light-years (10 parsecs) away. For example, the apparent brightness of our Sun is much greater than that of the star Rigel in the constellation Orion because it is so close to us. However, if both objects were placed at the same distance from us, Rigel would appear much brighter than our Sun because its absolute brightness is much larger.

Absolute Magnitude : The magnitude of an asteroid at zero phase angle and at unit heliocentric and geocentric distances. A measure of the intrinsic brightness (hence absolute) of a star. Defined to be equal to the apparent magnitude of a star if viewed from the standard distance of 10 parsecs. The difference between the observed apparent magnitude and the intrinsic absolute magnitude (assuming this is known from some other means) provides the distance to the star, through a formula known as the distance modulus. The symbol used for Absolute magnitude is the upper case letter M. The stellar magnitude any meteor would have if placed in the observer's zenith at a height of 100 km.

Absolute Zero : The coldest possible temperature, at which all molecular motion stops. On the Kelvin temperature scale, this temperature is the zero point (0 K), which is equivalent to –273° C and –460° F.

Absorption : The process by which light transfers its energy to matter. For example, a gas cloud can absorb starlight that passes through it. After the starlight passes through the cloud, dark lines called absorption lines appear in the star's continuous spectrum at wavelengths corresponding to the light-absorbing elements.

Absorption Line : A dark line in a continuous spectrum caused by absorption of light. Each chemical element emits and absorbs radiated energy at specific wavelengths, making it possible to identify the elements present in the atmosphere of a star or other celestial body by analyzing which absorption lines are present.

Absorption Lines : Dark lines superimposed over a bright continuous spectrum background, created when a cooler gas absorbs photons from a hotter source.

Accelerating Universe : A model for the universe in which a repulsive force counteracts the attractive force of gravity, driving all the matter in the universe apart at speeds that increase with time. Recent observations of distant supernova explosions suggest that we may live in an accelerating universe.

Access : The retrieval of information from whatever stores it, e.g. a chip, floppy disc or video tape (see also serial access and random access). Access time describes how long a system takes to find a given packet of data. As a verb it means to get access to. Access to a computer system may be open to anyone who knows who to work it; on the other hand, it may be controlled by formalities like subscriptions, logging-on procedures, passwords and so on.

Access Time : Describes how long a system takes to find a given item of data in backing store.

Accounts : An important area of business computing, in which the software greatly helps the keeping of accurate and up-to-date financial records.

Accretion : Accumulation of dust and gas into larger bodies.

Accretion Disk : A disk of gas which accumulates around a center of gravitational attraction, such as a white dwarf, neutron star, or black hole. As the gas spirals in, it becomes hot and emits light or even X-radiation.

Acoustic Coupler : This type of modem is designed as a cradle for a telephone handset linked to a computer through a cable. The coupler turns computer information into sound signals and vice versa. This method is not as fast as using a standard modem, and is sometimes unreliable, but couplers are cheap, portable and more flexible in use.

Active : Geomagnetic levels such that 15 is less than Ap which is less than 29.

Solar activity levels with at least one geophysical event or Several larger radio events (10cm) per day (Class M Flares)

Active Dark Filament (ADF) : An Active Prominence seen on the disk.

Active Galactic Nucleus (AGN) : The central region of an active galaxy where the energtic activity is concentrated. The active galactic nuclei are believed to contain supermassive black holes that power the nonstellar phenomena associated with active galaxies. A very bright, compact region found at the center of certain galaxies. The brightness of an active galactic nucleus is thought to come from an accretion disk around a supermassive black hole. The black hole devours matter from the accretion disk, and this infall of matter provides the firepower for quasars, the most luminous type of active galactic nucleus.

Active Galaxy : A galaxy possessing an active galactic nucleus at its center. Active Galaxies are galaxies characterized by certain properties: (1) High Luminosity, (2) Nonthermal Spectra that do not look like the sum of many stellar spectra, (3) Most of the luminosity is in a region of the spectrum other than optical (e.g., radio, UV, Infrared), (4) bright, star-like nucleus, (5) strong emission lines (most), (6) rapid variability, and sometimes (7) radio jets.

Active Longitude : The approximate center of a range of heliographic Longitudes in which Active Regions are more numerous and more Flare-active than the average.

Active Prominence : A Prominence displaying material motion and changes. In appearance over a few minutes of time.

Active Prominence Region (APR). A portion of the solar LIMB displaying. Active prominences.

A Ctive Region (AR) : A localized, transient volume of the solar atmosphere. In which plages, SUNSPOTS, faculae, flares, etc. May be observed.

Active Surge Region (ASR) : An Active Region that exhibits a group or Series of spike-like surges that rise above the limb.

ACU : Autodialler – automatic call unit.

Adams, John Couch : 1819-1892 English astronomer and mathematician who, at the age of 24, was the first person to predict the position of a planetary mass beyond Uranus. But, unfortunately, Adams did not publish his prediction. Galle confirmed the existence of Neptune based on independent calculations done by Le Verrier.

ADC : Analog to digital converter.

Address : A number, label or code that identifies a particular location in a computer memory or on a disc. Also a verb: a processor addresses a particular area when it directly reads information from it or writes to it.

Advanced Camera For Surveys (ACS) **:** An optical camera aboard the Hubble Space Telescope that covers twice the area, has twice the sharpness, and is up to ten times more efficient than the telescope's Wide Field and Planetary Camera 2. The camera's wavelength range spans from ultraviolet to near-infrared light. The camera's sharp eye and broader viewing area enable astronomers to study the life cycles of galaxies in the remotest regions of the cosmos. Astronauts installed the camera aboard the telescope in March 2002.

Aerial : A structure, also called antenna, that captures or transmits long electromagnetic waves – e.g. a television aerial and a mobile phone antenna.

Afterglow : The fading fireball of a gamma-ray burst — a sudden burst of gamma rays from deep space — that is observable in less energetic wavelengths, such as X-ray, optical, and radio. After an initial explosion, an expanding gamma-ray burst slows and sweeps up surrounding material, generating the afterglow, which is visible for several weeks or months. The afterglow is usually extremely faint, making it difficult to locate and study.

AI : Artificial intelligence.

Albedo : Reflectivity of an object; ratio of reflected light to incident light. The ratio of the amount of light reflected by an object and the amount of incident light; a measure of the reflectivity or intrinsic brightness of an object (a white, perfectly reflecting surface would have an albedo of 1.0; a black perfectly absorbing surface would have an albedo of 0.0).

Geometric albedo is the ratio of a body's brightness at zero phase angle to the brightness of a perfectly diffusing disk with the same position and apparent size as the body.

Albedo Feature : A dark or light marking on the surface of an object that may not be a geological or topographical feature.

Albumin : The most prevalent protein found in blood It is used as a stabilizer in the manufacturing process of several factor VIII therapies.

Algorithm : A way to describe the method of solving a problem as a logical series of steps; may be in words, as a chart, or in pseudocode.

Allocthonous : Material that is formed or introduced from somewhere other than the place it is presently found.

Fragmented rock thrown out of the crater during its formation that either falls back to partly fill the crater or blankets its outer flanks after the impact event.

Alpha Centauri : The closest bright star to our solar system.

Alpha Process : A process by which lighter elements capture helium nuclei (alpha particles) to form heavier elements. For example, when a carbon nucleus captures an alpha particle, a heavier oxygen nucleus is formed.

Alphanumeric : An alphanumeric character is any letter, number or symbol on a keyboard. The US form is alphanumeric.

Altitude : The angular distance from the observer's horizon, usually taken to be that horizon that is unobstructed by natural or artificial features (such as mountains or buildings), measured directly up from the horizon toward the zenith; positive numbers indicate values of altitude above the horizon, and negative numbers indicate below the horizon — with negative numbers usually being used in terms of how far below the horizon the sun is situated at a given time [for example, the boundary between civil twilight and nautical twilight is when the sun is at altitude -6 degrees]

AM : Amplitude modulation.

Amplifier : A device to increase the strength (amplitude) of an analogue signal.

Technical word for signal size, with the amplitude of a signal relating to its strength.

Amplitude : The size of a wave from the top of a wave crest to its midpoint.

Amplitude Modulation (AM) : Method of encoding an information signal on to a carrier wave by varying the amplitude.

An area seen as a dark spot on the photosphere of the Sun; sunspots are concentrations of magnetic flux, typically occurring in bipolar clusters or groups; they appear dark because they are cooler than the surrounding photosphere.

Analog : Refers to many real world quantities (e.g. time, temperature, pressure, weight) that vary smoothly in value, rather than in the steps of digital (numeric) form. Digital computers can handle such information only by assigning numbers to it. This usually means translating it into bits, binary 0s and 1s.

Analog to Digital Converter (ADC) : A type of device for converting analog information (e.g. of time or temperature) into digital form. Such converters allow digital hardware to link to analog systems.

Andromeda Galaxy : The Andromeda galaxy is the largest of the local galaxies, and is visible to the unaided eye. It is about 2 million light years from our own galaxy and has a beautiful spiral structure. The Andromeda galaxy is also known as M31. The Andromeda galaxy and the Milky Way galaxy will eventually collide.

Angstrom : A unit of length = 1.0E-10E^{-08} cm o 10^{-10} m

Angular Momentum : A property that an object, such as a planet revolving around the Sun, possesses by virtue of its rotation or circular motion. An object's angular momentum cannot change unless some force acts to speed up or slow down its circular motion. This principle, known as conservation of angular momentum, is why an object can indefinitely maintain a circular motion around an axis of revolution or rotation.

Angular Resolution : The ability of an instrument, such as a telescope, to distinguish objects that are very close to each other. The angular resolution of an instrument is the smallest angular separation at which the instrument can observe two neighboring objects as two separate objects The angular resolution of the human eye is about a minute of arc. As car headlights approach from a far-off point, they appear as a single light until the separation between the lights increases to a point where they can be resolved as two separate lights.

Angular Size : The apparent size of an object as seen by an observer; expressed in units of degrees (of arc), arc minutes, or arc seconds. The moon, as viewed from the Earth, has an angular diameter of one-half a degree.

Animation : The arrangement of a sequence of separate pictures, e.g. video frames and computer graphics, made to follow each other so quickly they appear to the viewer as continuous movement.

Answer Back : Special code sent by a telex machine, for instance, to show that a message has been received.

Antenna : Aerial.

Antimatter : Matter made up of elementary particles whose masses are identical to their normal-matter counterparts but whose other properties, such as electric charge, are reversed. The positron is the antimatter counterpart of an electron, with a positive charge instead of a negative charge. When an antimatter particle collides with its normal-matter counterpart, both particles are annihilated and energy is released.

Antipodal point : The point that is directly on the opposite side of the planet; e.g., the Earth's north pole is antipodal to its south pole.

Ap INDEX : An averaged planetary A INDEX based on data from a set of specific Stations.

Aperture : The size of the primary optical surface of an astronomical instrument (telescope), usually given in inches, centimeters, or meters. In the case of a reflecting telescope, the aperture usually refers to the size of the main mirror; in the case of a refracting telescope (of which binoculars are one example), the aperture refers to the size of the primary lens (which in binoculars is usually given in millimeters).

Aperture Card : A type of microform, in which a large card carries a single frame in a central hole.

Aphelion : The point in its orbit where a planet is farthest from the sun; when refering to objects orbiting the earth the term **apogee** is used; the term **apoapsis** is used for orbits around other bodies. (opposite of perihelion)

Aphelion distance : abbr. Q, distance of greatest heliocentric separation for a body in an eccentric orbit; $Q=a(1+e)$.

Apoapsis : The point in orbit farthest from the planet.

The furthest point of a planet or moon to the star or planet it's orbiting. Since all astronomical bodies are moving, objects orbiting them have slightly elliptical orbits.

The point in orbit farthest from the Earth.

Apollo asteroids : Asteroids having semimajor axes $a>1.0$ au, and perihelion distances $q<1.017$ au.

Apparent Brightness (Apparent Magnitude) **:** A measure of the brightness of a celestial object as it appears from Earth. The Sun is the brightest object in Earth's sky and has the greatest apparent magnitude, with the moon second. Apparent brightness does not take into account how far away the object is from Earth.

Apparent Magnitude : The brightness of a star as it *appears* to the eye or to the telescope, as measured in units of magnitude. The symbol used for apparent magnitude is the lower case letter m.

Applications Programme : Software that applies a computer to a real world problem such as handling accounts or driving a robot.

Arago, Dominique François Jean 1786 - 1853 **:** French astronomer and physicist and Director of the Paris Observatory, who discovered the phenomenon of the production of magnetism by rotation

Arc minutes : There are 60 minutes (denoted as 60') of arc in 1 degree. In the sky, with an unobstructed horizon (as on the ocean), one can see about 180 degrees of sky at once, and there are 90 degrees from the true horizon to the zenith. The full moon is about 30' (30 arc minutes) across, or half a degree. There are 60 seconds (denoted 60") of arc in one minute of arc.

Arc Second : One arc second is 1/60 of an arc minute and 1/3600 of an arc degree. The apparent size of a dime about 3.7 kilometers (2.3 miles) away would be an arc second. The angular diameter of Jupiter varies from about 30 to 50 arc seconds, depending on its distance from Earth.

Arch Filament System (AFS). A bright, compact PLAGE crossed by a system of Small, arched FILAMENTS, which is often a sign of rapid or contin- Ued growth in an ACTIVE REGION.

Architecture : The logical (effective) layout of a circuit, system or cable network.

Archive : A form of data held to meet long-term needs (perhaps for reference), that will not need to be changed.

Arcuate : Having the form of a bow; curved; arc-shaped

Argument of Perihelion : The angle (in the body's orbit plane) between the ascending node line and perihelion measured in the direction of the body's orbit.

Array : A list or table of numbers or words laid out in an orderly way to allow easy access; a form of network.

Arthropathy : Chronic joint disease (arthritis) caused by repeated and uncontrolled bleeding into joints. This is the leading cause of disability in people living with hemophilia.

Artificial Intelligence (AI) : Some computer software displays intelligence in the sense that, if humans were to perform the same task, you would describe them as intelligent. For example, an AI programme may add to its 'knowledge' from previous runs; interpret the meaning of a question from its context; prove mathematical theorems; or diagnose diseases or electronic faults. Machine intelligence is sometimes the phrase used (see also expert systems).

Artwork : Originally, graphics in a form ready for printing, but now often used for any kind of material ready for printing.

ASCII : American Standard Code for Information Interchange: an internationally accepted system for coding characters for processing and transfer. For instance, the ASCII code for the letter 'A' is 65 (in base 10) while that for 'B' is 66. (In binary form these codes are 0100 0001 and 0100 0010 respectively.)

Ash : The fine-grained material produced by a pyroclastic eruption. An ash particle is defined to have a diameter of less than 2 millimeters.

Aspect Ratio : The ratio of the width to the height of a single frame or screen. For instance, video pictures are four units wide to three high, while film and 35 mm transparencies are three units wide to two high. Most media have the same aspect ratio as television sets, though standard paper is 7.1 units wide to 10 high.

Aspic : One of several systems for coding layout and heading instructions so that a disc containing word processed text can be inserted directly into a typesetting machine to produce camera-ready pages.

Assembler : A programme that translates assembly language instructions into machine code.

Assembly Language : A low level programming language that uses coded versions of English words to give instructions to a processor. The assembler automatically translates these into machine language. Assembly language is harder for humans to work with than high level programming languages like Basic.

Asterism : An easily recognizable mini-constellation that allows you to easily spot the remainder of the constellation. The Big Dipper in Ursa Major (the Great Bear) is an example of an asterism, as is the Great Square in Pegasus.

Asteroid : An asteroid is a planetesirnal in orbit around the sun. Generally, asteroids are rocky bodies concentrated in orbits between Mars and Jupiter. The largest known asteroid is 1 Ceres which is about 933 km (~580 mi) in diameter.

One of a number of objects ranging in size from sub-km to about 1000 km, most of which lie between the orbits of Mars and Jupiter; also called 'minor planet'. The preliminary designations consist of the year of discovery, an upper case letter to indicate the halfmonth in that year (A=Jan 1-15, B=Jan 16-31, ..., Y=Dec 16-31, the letter I being omitted), and a second upper case letter in sequence. When this sequence of 25 letters (with I again being omitted) has been completed it is repeated and followed by a sequential number. Permanent designations consist of numbers and names, beginning with (1) Ceres, given to asteroids for which orbits are accurately determined. Names are generally proposed by the discoverer.

Small, rocky bodies that orbit the Sun, asteroids range in diameter from a few millimeters to over 250 km. Although all asteriods reflect sunlight, only one, Vesta, can be seen with the unaided eye.

Asteroid Belt : A region of space between Mars and Jupiter where the great majority of asteroids is found.

Astrometry : Astrometry pertains to the measurement of the position in the sky of solar-system bodies. Position measurements are typically made in right ascension and declination. The careful, precise measurement of astronomical objects, usually made with respect to standard catalogues of star positions. For comet orbit computations, astrometry good to 1" or 2" (1 or 2 arc seconds), or better, is the standard nowadays.

Astronomer : A scientist who studies the universe and the celestial bodies that reside in it, including their composition, history, location, and motion. Many of the scientists at the Space Telescope Science Institute are astronomers. Astronomers from all over the world use the Hubble Space Telescope. An expert in the study of the Sun, Moon, stars, planets, and other space bodies.

Astronomical Unit (AU) : 149,597,870.691 km; the average distance from the Earth to the Sun. 1 AU is a long way — at 100 miles per hour (160 kph) it would take over 100 years to go 1 AU. Approximately equal to the mean earth-sun distance, which is about 150,000,000 km or 93,000,000 miles. Formally, the AU is actually slightly less than the earth's mean distance from the sun (semi-major axis) because it is the radius of a circular orbit of negligible mass (and unperturbed by other planets) that revolves about the sun in a specific period of time.

The average distance between the Earth and the Sun, one astronomical unit is defined to be 150 million kilometers, or about 93 million miles.

The average distance between the Earth and the Sun, which is about 150 million kilometers (93 million miles). This unit of length is commonly used for measuring the distances between objects within the solar system.

The average distance from the Earth to the Sun; 1 AU is 149,597,870 kilometers (92,960,116 miles).

The mean earth-sun distance, equal to 1.496E+13cm Or 214.94 solar radii.

The approximate distance from the Sun to the Earth which is equal to 150,000,000 kilometers.

Astrophysics : The branch of astronomy that deals with the physics of stellar phenomena.

The study of the history, structure and dynamics of objects in the universe. Astrophysicists study stars, solar systems and interstellar material.

Asymptotic Giant Branch : The part of the HR diagram (in the upper right hand corner) where stars move to after Helium burning ceases in their cores. The carbon core of the star shrinks, the outer layers expand, and the star becomes a large red giant.

Aten Asteroids : Asteroids having semimajor axes $a<1.0$ au, and aphelion distances $Q>0.983$ au.

ATM : Automatic teller machine.

Atmosphere : = 1.013 bars = 1.03 kg/cm^2 = 14.7 pounds per square inch, standard atmospheric pressure at sea level on Earth.

One atmosphere is 14.7 pounds per square inch (10^5 Newtons per square meter); the average atmospheric pressure at sea level on Earth.

The air (gases) that surrounds the Earth or any heavenly body

The layer of gases surrounding the surface of a planet, moon, or star.

The layers of gases which surround a star, like our Sun, or a planet, like our Earth.

Atom : The smallest unit of matter that possesses chemical properties. All atoms have the same basic structure: a nucleus containing positively charged protons with an equal number of negatively charged electrons orbiting around it. In addition to protons, most nuclei contain neutral neutrons whose mass is similar to that of protons. Each atom corresponds to a unique chemical element determined by the number of protons in its nucleus.

Atomic Nucleus : The positively charged core of an atom consisting of protons and (except for hydrogen) neutrons, and around which electrons orbit.

Attenuation : Loss of strength of a signal while it travels over a distance, as in a sound getting fainter with distance from the source.

AU : AU is short for Astronomical Unit and defined as: the radius of an unperturbed circular orbit around the Sun of a massless body having an orbital period of 2*(pi)/k days (k is the Gaussian gravitational constant). One AU is slightly less than the average distance between the Earth and the Sun (approximately 1.5x10^11 m).

Audio : Concerns sound waves in the audible frequency range (roughly 20 Hz to 20,000 Hz), or electrical signals in the same range and equipment to handle them.

Audit Trail : A printout report produced by some accounts software that shows what happens to a set of transactions.

Aurora : (Latin for "dawn") a glow in a planet's ionosphere caused by the interaction between the planet's magnetic field and charged particles from the Sun

A glow in a planet's ionosphere caused by the interaction between the planet's magnetic field and charged particles from the Sun.

A phenomenon produced when the solar wind (made up of energized electrons and protons) disturbs the atoms and molecules in a planet's upper atmosphere. Some of the energy produced by these disturbances is converted into colorful visible light, which shimmers and dances. Auroras have been seen on several planets in our solar system. On Earth, auroras are also known as the "Northern Lights" (aurora borealis) or "Southern Lights" (aurora australis), depending on in which polar region they appear.

Aurora Borealis : The "Northern Lights"; caused by the interaction between the solar wind, the Earth's magnetic field and the upper atmosphere. A similar effect happens in the southern hemisphere where it is known as the aurora australis.

Aurora: A faint visual phenomenon associated with geomagnetic activity, Which occurs mainly in the high-latitude night sky; typical Auroras are 100 to 250 km above the ground.

Auroral Oval : An oval band around each geomagnetic pole which is the locus. Of structured aurorae.

Authoring Language : A very high level programming language designed to speed up and simplify the job of writing applications software for computer-based systems. Authoring (or author) languages may also have special editing facilities and software tools to enable people who are not professional programmers to write their own software, e.g. for training; they are then sometimes called authoring systems. People often use modern authoring software for the control of presentation systems that include video tape or video disc.

Autodial : A facility allowing automatic calling of telephone numbers that have previously been stored, on receipt of simple codes. The device that offers the feature is an autodialler, or automatic call unit (ACU).

Automation : Putting processes under the control of machines rather than of people; this includes robotics.

Autumnal Equinox : The equinox that occurs in September.

The place in the sky where the Sun crosses the celestial equator moving southwards. The autumnal equinox marks the beginning of autumn and falls on, or near, September 21. See celestial sphere for a helpful diagram.

AXIS : An imaginary straight line around which an object rotates.

Azimuth : The angular distance of an object, measured eastward, from north. 0° is due north, 90° is due east, 180° is due south, and 270° is due west.

Angular distance measured clockwise around the observer's horizon in units of degrees; astronomers usually take north to be 0 degrees, east to be 90 degrees, south to be 180 degrees, and west to be 270 degrees.

❑❑❑

B

Background : A processor can divide its attention so as to do several jobs at the same time. The simplest form of this time-sharing is where one job (like a spreadsheet) is worked on 'in the foreground' while another (like printing out some text) takes place whenever there are no other demands on the processor, i.e. in the background.

Backing : Backing store is external memory that supports and communicates with a computer's internal memory. Back-up equipment duplicates crucial items in case of breakdown. Thus people keep back-up discs in case of loss of or damage to the originals. To back-up a disc is to copy it in its entirety.

BACTERIA : Living things that have only one cell and are so small they can only be seen with a microscope.

Bandwidth : A measure of the information-carrying capacity of a communication channel. The higher the frequencies used, the more bandwidth may be available (see also broadband and narrowband).

Bar : = 0.987 atmosphere = 1.02 kg/cm^2 = 100 kilopascal = 14.5 lbs/square inch.

A unit of pressure, equal to the sea-level pressure of Earth's atmosphere; 1 bar = 0.987 atmosphere = 101,300 pascals = 14.5 lbs/square inch = 100,000 Newtons per square meter.

Bar Code : A pattern of printed lines (often seen on library books and items for sale) used for direct input of data to a computer with a bar code reader.

Barnard, Edward Emerson 1857-1923 : American astronomer; discovered Jupiter's satellite Amalthea and Barnard's star, the second-nearest star system to the Sun.

Barred Spiral Galaxy : A galaxy with a "bar" of stars and interstellar matter, such as dust and gas, slicing across its center. The Milky Way is thought to be a barred spiral galaxy.

Barsoom : The local name for Mars in Edgar Rice Burroughs' SF books.

Bartel's Rotation Number : The serial number assigned to 27-day rotation. Periods of solar and geophysical parameters. Rotation 1 in this. Sequence was assigned arbitrarily by Bartel to begin in January 1833.

Barycenter : The center of mass of a system of bodies, such as the solar system. When a comet, for example, is well outside the orbit of Neptune (the farthest major planet), it sees the sun and major planets essentially as a single object of summed mass, and the center of this mass (called the barycenter of the solar system) is offset somewhat from the sun; "original" and "future" orbits of long-period comets are computed for this barycenter, while perturbed, osculating orbits of currently-observed objects in the inner solar system are computed for heliocentric orbits.

Barycentric Dynamical Time (TDB) : Differing from TDT only via periodic variations, TDB is used in ephemerides and equations of motion that refer to the barycenter of the solar system.

Basalt : A dark, fine-grained volcanic rock.

A general term for dark-colored, igneous rocks composed of minerals that are relatively rich in iron and magnesium.

Base Station : The unit in a cellular telephone network that handles the calls within a small area (cell).

Baseline : The distance between two or more telescopes that are working together as a single instrument to observe celestial objects. The wider the baseline, the greater the resolving power.

Basic : Beginners' All-purpose Symbolic Instruction Code: a very popular high level programming language, almost universally available on microcomputers, but in many incompatible dialects.

Batch Processing : A style of computer processing in which various jobs are run in one batch, the opposite of interactive processing.

Batching : Collecting together all messages for one destination and sending them off at the same time.

BATSE (Burst and Transient Source Experiment) : A high-energy astrophysics "experiment" used to investigate gamma-ray bursts (grbs). BATSE consisted of eight detectors that were mounted on the corners of NASA's Earth-orbiting Compton Gamma-Ray Observatory, whose mission ended in 2000.

Baud : A unit of rate of transfer of information within or between systems. Thus telex operates at 50 baud; programmes often load from cassettes at 300 baud; teletex operates at 1200 or 2400 baud. For most practical purposes, one baud is one bit per second.

Baudot : The well established information communications code used in telegraphy and telex, with a five-bit word length.

Bepposax : A space-based X-ray observatory built and operated by the Italian Space Agency and the Netherlands Agency for Aerospace Programs. Bepposax has been instrumental in identifying and locating gamma-ray bursts.

Bespoke : Describes a system that is designed for a particular customer. Commissioning bespoke software is the opposite approach to buying a package off the shelf.

Besselian Year : A quantity introduced by F. W. Bessel in the nineteenth century that has been used into the twentieth century. Bessel introduced a system whereby it would be convenient to identify any instant of time by giving the year and the decimal fraction of the year to a few places, but the starting time of the year was not convenient for dynamical studies that utilize Julian dates (see definition for Julian date), differing by 0.5 day, and the Besselian year varies slowly. The recent change to Julian year usage in dynamical astronomy (and the J2000.0 equinox) took effect in solar-system ephemerides of the Minor Planet Center and Central Bureau for Astronomical Telegrams on Jan. 1, 1992. (See Julian year.)

Big Bang : A broadly accepted theory for the origin and evolution of our universe. The theory says that the observable universe started roughly 15 billion years ago from an extremely dense and incredibly hot initial state.

The state of extremely high (classically, infinite) density and temperature from which the universe began expanding. The beginning point of time and space for the universe.

Big Bang Nucleosynthesis : Lighter elements, such as Hydrogen, Helium and Lithium, were formed as a result of the big bang in a process called big bang nucleosynthesis. Scientists can calculate how much of which elements were formed, and the fact that observation agrees with calculation is considered proof of the big bang theory.

Big Bang Theory : A theory which states that the Universe began to expand after a super powerful explosion of concentrated matter and energy.

The widely held belief that the Universe began in a fiery explosion, 10-15 billion years ago. The cosmic microwave background, big bang nucleosynthesis, and the observed Hubble expansion of the Universe are considered proof of the big bang theory.

For more on big bang cosmology, check out this primer.

Billion : The American version of "billion" means 1,000,000,000 (1e9); whreas the British version means 1e12.

Binary Number : A number written in the binary system, so built up only from the digits 0 and 1.

Binary Star System : A system of two stars orbiting around a common center of mass that are bound together by their mutual gravitational attraction. While some instances of "optical doubles" exist, most stars are, in fact, found in pairs orbiting around a common centre of mass. Such stars may be discovered optically (visual binaries) if they are well separated, by the orbital radial velocities of one or two (single or double-line spectroscopic binaries) or by their varying light curves (eclipsing binaries). Binaries are of immense importance in astronomy because they provide our only direct source of measurement of stellar masses.

Binary System : A method of counting which uses only two digits (0 and 1) instead of the usual 10 (0 to 9); digital computers work in binary deep down in effect.

Bioelectronics : Such technology uses microelectronics circuits with biological materials or with biological systems. Thus a biosensor is a sensor that handles some physiological input, such as blood sugar content.

Bit : A binary digit, 0 or 1.

BL Lac Object (also Blazar) **:** A type of active galaxy characterized by very rapid (day to day) variability by large percentages in total luminosity, no emission lines, strong nonthermal radiation, and starlike appearance. A BL Lac object is a radio galaxy aligned so that we are looking down the jet into the very heart of the system, right into the nucleus. Since we are looking right along the jet we see very rapid, highly luminous radiation.

Black Body : An ideal object that is a perfect absorber of light (hence the name since it would appear completely black if it were cold), and also a perfect emitter of light. Light is emitted by solid objects because those objects are composed of atoms and molecules which can emit and absorb light. They emit light because they are wiggling around due to their heat content (thermal energy). So a blackbody emits a certain spectrum of light that depends only on its temperature. The higher the temperature, the more light energy is emitted and the higher the frequency (shorter-the wavelength) of the peak of the spectrum.

Black Body Radiation : The thermal radiation that would be emitted from a black body (an object that reflects no incoming radiation) at a particular temperature.

Black Body Temperature : The temperature of an object if it is reradiating all the thermal energy that has been added to it; if an object is not a blackbody radiator, it will not reradiate all the excess heat and the leftover will go toward increasing its temperature.

Black Hole : A black hole is an extreme curvature of space time created by a highly concentrated mass. It may be "seen" by the radiation emitted by infalling material (the accretion disk) prior to crossing the event horizon. Black holes have two key structural components: the "photon sphere", a region in space-time such that any light falling within the photon sphere from an outside source is trapped; and the "event horizon" the radius (2/3 that of the photon sphere) from which nothing, including light, can escape. A black hole of 1 solar mass has an event horizon of 3 km. Radius and a photon sphere of 4.5 km. Radius. The radii are directly proportional to the mass. Black holes are believed to be formed in the explosion of very massive stars (> 10 solar masses), perhaps in the early universe in the Big Bang model, and in the centres of many galaxies. It is important to remember that the gravitational effect of a black hole is the same at a large distance as that of any object of equal mass. Thus, if the Sun were somehow to turn into a black hole, the orbit of the Earth would not really be affected.

Black-Body Radiation : A "black-body" is an ideal object whose temperature is the same at every point and constant in time. It is useful for study because such an object produces a spectrum which is dependent only on the temperature. The spectrum of b-b radiation is continuous from zero energy at zero wavelength, rising to a maximum at some wavelength determined by Wien's law, and then falling off to zero at infinite wavelength. The hotter the black body, the more energy is produced at EVERY wavelength. Black-bodies are useful models because many stars radiate approximately as b-b.

Blue Star : A massive, hot star that appears blue in color. Spica in the constellation Virgo is an example of a blue star.

Blueshift : The shortening of a light wave from an object moving toward an observer. For example, when a star is traveling toward Earth, its light appears bluer.

Board : A circuit and a set of chips on a printed circuit board, added to a hardware device to provide extra features.

Bode, Johann Elert 1747-1826 **:** German astronomer, known for the bogus "Bode's Law" which attempts to explain the sizes of the planetary orbits.

Body Awareness : A person's feelings and attitudes about his or her body; the mental picture of one's body – its existence, position in space, and parts in relation to each other. Other people's reactions to one's appearance influence the way one feels about one's body.

Bolide : Large, brilliant meteors that enter the Earth's atmosphere. Friction between a fast-moving meteor and Earth's air molecules generates tremendous heat, which causes the meteor to heat up, glow, and perhaps disintegrate. In some cases, the meteor literally explodes, leaving a visible cloud that dissipates slowly.

Bolometric Magnitude : The magnitude that a star would have if all of its energetic emissions were included in the measurement. For example when you look at a star and observe its brightness with your eye, your eye is only detecting the brightness from the visible portion of the spectrum. If your eye could see into the ultraviolet the star might appear much brighter. The bolometric magnitude is the estimate of how bright the star would be if all of its light, from the entire spectrum, was observed.

Bombardment : To strike with fast moving objects such as meteorites

Bond, William Cranch 1789-1859 : One of the earliest American astronomers of note; rose from poverty and overcame a lack of formal education to become the first director of the Harvard College Observatory where he studied Saturn and (with Lassell) discovered its moon Hyperion.

Boot : Programmes can be made to load and run automatically on switch-on, so the system boots itself—'pulls itself up by its bootstraps'.

Bow shock : The outermost part of a planetary magnetosphere; the place where the supersonic flow of the solar wind is slowed to subsonic speed by the planetary magnetic field.

BPS : Bits per second, a measure of information transfer rate (see also baud).

Brahe, Tycho 1546-1601 : (a.k.a Tyge Ottesen) Danish astronomer whose accurate astronomical observations formed the basis for Johannes Kepler's laws of planetary motion.

Branching : A method of passing through a course, programme or database by a route that depends on inputs, rather than by a fixed route (linear).

Breccia : A course-grained rock, composed of angular, broken rock fragments held together by a mineral cement or a fine-grained matrix.

Bridge : A hardware and software link between, for instance, two networks.

Bright surge on the limb (bsd) : A large gaseous stream (SURGE) that moves Outward more than 0.15 solar radius above the LIMB.

Brightness : Like flux brightness is energy per unit time per unit area (e.g. Ergs per second per square centimeter). How bright something appears to you depends on how much energy (light) it is giving off per second, and how spread out it is over your viewing area. A certain amount of light energy will appear much brighter if concentrated into a small region of emission than when spread out over a large emission region. A tiny lightbulb can seem very bright, even when its total light is small. The apparent brightness of a star is called the apparent magnitude and that is what is measured by a telescope: how much energy does the star put into the telescope's collecting area per second. British astronomer who discovered Uranus and cataloged more than 800 double stars and 2,500 nebulae.

British Telecom (BT) : The United Kingdom's main telecommunication system provider.

British Telecom Gold (BTG) : A major British interactive viewdata base, with a strong electronic mail component.

Broadband (Wideband) : Describes a communications channel with plenty of bandwidth, usually taken to mean at least enough to transmit television signals at normal speed (contrast narrowband).

Broadcast : A process of distributing signals one-way to a wide audience, often by radio or television, usually financed by some blanket method of payment or advertising (contrast narrowcast).

Broadcast Videotex : Teletext.

Brown dwarf : An object between 0.013 and 0.080 solar masses (13 to 80 Jupiter-masses): too small for normal nuclear fusion but big enough to fuse deuterium. Brown dwarfs are larger than planets but smaller than stars. An object too samll to be an ordinary star because produce enough energy by fusion in its core to compensate for the radiative energy to loses from its surface. A brown dward has a mass less than 0.08 times that of the Sun.

Bubble Memory : A compact and robust form of main memory which depends on storing information in magnetic 'bubbles' (domains) in a thin film of a material like garnet.

Bubbling : An unusual, intermittent feeling in a joint or muscle that indicates early stages of bleeding.

Buffer : A temporary store for information in transfer, e.g. for holding a text until a printer has completed the printout, thus releasing the processor for other tasks.

Bug : A mistake, in a system or programme removed by debugging.

Building Trust : Developing a comfort level with a group through interactions that encourage positive risk-taking.

Bulge : The spherical structure at the center of a spiral galaxy that is made up primarily of old stars, gas, and dust. The Milky Way's bulge is roughly 15,000 light-years across.

Bulge, Galactic : A thick region around the center of the Galaxy that spheroidal in shape, containing warm gas and metal-rich older stars.

Bulletin Board : A communal electronic notice board that allows people to log on and exchange news, views, for sale notices, and wants. Some bulletin boards are commercial, while others are run by hobbyists. They can be a cross between magazine, notice board, and exchange and mart system.

Bureau : An agency that offers special high power services to a number of firms that can't afford, or don't need, to own the systems involved themselves.

Burst : A transient enhancement of the solar radio emission, usually Associated with an active region or flare.

Bus : A common path that links all the different parts of a computer system, such as a network allowing them to exchange data. Everything is linked to the bus at all times, but each device takes data from the bus, or puts data on to it, only when necessary.

Butte : A conspicuous, isolated, flattop hill with steep slopes.

Byte : A byte, a group of eight bits, can represent any keyboard character or control code. An eight-bit processor handles information in bytes (still sometimes called octets), therefore, and machines with more power deal with data in pairs of bytes or even larger groups.

❑❑❑

C

Cable : Describes video distributed through wires rather than broadcast using radio waves. In areas with poor reception, a cable operator may erect a high performance antenna and distribute the signal by cable to people. A cable network over an area may offer a whole new approach to many kinds of electronic information transfer (see also closed circuit TV).

CAD : Computer-aided design.

Calcium K : A narrow wavelength of blue light which is emitted and absorbed by ions of the element calcium.

Caldera : Crater formed by an explosion or collapse of a volcanic vent. Lrge, basin-shaped volcanic depression that is more or less circular in form. Most volcanic calderas are produced by collapse of the roof of a magma chamber due to removal of magma by voluminous eruptions or subterranean withdrawal of the magma, although some calderas may be formed by explosive removal of the upper part of a volcano.

Call Logger : A unit that monitors a telephone system and keeps details of all calls made for later study.

CAM : Computer-aided manufacture.

Camera-ready : Describes material in a form suited for printing (by a process camera).

Capacitance : Ability to store electric charge; in some video disc systems, the varying capacitance between the pick-up (head) and the disc's data surface codes audio and video information.

Caption Camera : A video camera with the function of sending signals that represent captions to a mixer.

Carbon/oxygen white dwarf : Stars like the Sun, while massive enough to fuse He, will not be able to reach the core conditions (600 million K) to fuse carbon or oxygen, the next possible fuel. Thus their shell sources remain the only source of fusion energy, turning H into He and He into C and O as they contract. Thus the end state of such a star is a white dwarf primarily composed of C and O.

Carbonaceous Chondrite : A meteorite with embedded pebble-sized granules that contain significant quantities of organic (complex carbon-rich) matter.

Carbonate : A compound containing carbon and oxygen (i.e. Calcium carbonate a.k.a. Limestone).

Card : Board, but see also punched media and stripe card.

Carousel : A system that cycles again and again through a series of pictures or viewdata frames.

Carrier Wave : A wave (often of light or radio) which carries an information signal by the variations of some kind (for instance, of amplitude or frequency) imposed on it.

Carriers : Persons who possess and can pass a recessive gene to their offspring, but do not express the trait themselves. Because hemophilia is an X-linked, recessive trait, females are carriers of hemophilia but are seldom affected.

Carrington Longitude : A system of fixed longitudes rotating with the sun.

Cartridge : Software on ROM for some microcomputers is sold as a sealed plug-in cartridge. It is then easier to use than if on disc, or on a ROM without the cartridge.

Cassini, Giovanni Domenico 1625-1712 : (a.k.a. Jean Dominique) Italian-born French astronomer and first director of the Royal Observatory in Paris; discoverer of four of Saturn's moons (Tethys, Dione, Rhea and Iapetus) and the major division in its rings.

Cataclastic : A texture found in metamorphic rocks in which brittle minerals have been broken, crushed and flattened during shearing.

Catalogue : The place on a disc that carries a list of its contents; also called directory.

Catena : A chain of craters.

Cathode Ray Tube (CRT) : In this device a narrow controlled beam of high energy electrons puts a visible picture of some kind on its screen. Monitors, TV sets and radar displays are based on the CRT.

Cauzon Strip : Data for a computer, printed in robust and compact form on paper for reading by a special input device.

Cavus : Hollows, irregular depressions.

CCD : Charge-coupled device, a very sensitive electronic device that is revolutionizing astronomy in the 1990s. CCD cameras are composed of silicon chips that are sensitive to light, changing detected photons of light into electronic signals that can then be used to make images of astronomical objects or to analyze how much light is being received from such objects. Ccds require computers for reduction of data, so the expense can be much greater than for, say, photography — but ccds can detect much fainter objects than can photographs. Unfiltered ccds tend to be more red-sensitive than the human eye.

CCITT : International Consultative Committee for Telephony and Telegraphy: a body that issues standards for telecommunications and data transfer for most countries outside the USA.

CCTV : Closed circuit television.

CD : Compact disc: CD-I is compact disc interactive; CD-ROM is compact disc read-only memory.

Ceefax : A teletext service provided by the British Broadcasting Corporation.

Celestial Equator : An imaginary line around the sky directly above the equator. See celestial sphere for a helpful diagram.

Celestial sphere : An imaginary sphere of great (or infinite) radius that is centered on the earth and is used for practical purposes in astronomical observing. Since stars (other than our own sun!) Are very distant from us, they make up a background that is essentially unchanging from year to year; of course, over a period of years, the closer stars will move very slightly and factors such as precession cause a change in the appearance of the stars in our skies over many years. But we create a map grid on the celestial sphere for identifying, referring to, and locating objects in the sky; some of these map grids include equatorial coordinates (right ascension and declination), ecliptic coordinates (ecliptic longitude and latitude), and galactic coordinates (galactic longitude and latitude) — which refer to the earth's rotation, the earth's revolution about the sun, and the Milky Way galaxy's plane, respectively.

Celestial Sphere: A huge sphere centered on the Earth, which provides a convenient way to fix a coordinate system on the sky. Every object in the sky can be found by knowing its declination and right ascension.

An imaginary sphere encompassing the Earth that represents the sky. Astronomers chart the sky using the celestial coordinates of the sphere to locate objects in the cosmos. This sphere is divided into 88 sections called constellations. Objects are sometimes named for the major constellation in which they appear.

Cell : A particular item in an array—e.g., a data site in a spreadsheet a unit of the picture on a screen (pixel), an area serviced by one transmitter in a radio telephone system.

Celsius (Centigrade) Temperature Scale : Temperature scale on which the freezing point of water is 0° C and the boiling point is 100° C.

A scale on a thermometer where the interval between the boiling point and the freezing point of water is divided into 100 degrees. Freezing point is represented by 0 degrees and boiling point is represented by 100 degrees. The same scale is also utilized in Centigrade.

Centigrade : See CELSIUS.

Centimeter Burst : A solar radio burst in the centimeter wavelength range.

Central peak : The exposed core of uplifted rocks in complex meteorite impact craters; the central peak material typically shows evidence of intense fracturing, faulting and shock metamorphism.

Central Processing Unit (CPU) : Processor.

Cepheid Variable : A type of pulsating star whose light and energy output vary noticeably over a set period of time. The time period over which the star varies is directly related to its light output or luminosity, making these stars useful standard candles for measuring intergalactic distances.

A type of luminous giant star whose luminosity varies in a periodic fashion. Cepheids are characterized by a rapid rise in luminosity followed by a slow decline. The period of the cycle is related to the luminosity of the Cepheid by the Period-Luminosity relationship. The more luminous the Cepheid, the longer the period. This property makes Cepheids useful for obtaining distances. Cepheids come in two types, Type I which are metal rich and Type II which are metal poor. Type I Cepheids are more luminous than Type II.

Chandra X-Ray Observatory : A space-based X-ray observatory; also known as the Advanced X-ray Astrophysics Facility (AXAF). Chandra is designed to observe X-rays from high-energy regions of the universe, such as hot gas in the remnants of exploded stars. The satellite was launched and deployed in July 1999.

Chandrasekhar Mass : The maximum mass, approximately 1.4 solar masses above which an object has too much mass to support itself against collapse by electron degeneracy pressure. Hence, the maximum mass of a white dwarf.

Chaos : Distinctive area of broken terrain.

Character : Any number, letter, symbol or control code on a keyboard, screen or printer, the collection of all symbols that a system can process or display being its character set.

Charge-Coupled Device (CCD) : An electronic detector that records visible light from stars and galaxies to make photographs. These detectors are very sensitive to the extremely faint light of distant galaxies. They can see objects that are 1,000 million times fainter than the eye can see. Ccds are electronic circuits composed of light-sensitive picture elements (pixels), tiny cells that, placed together, resemble mesh on a screen door. The same CCD technology is used in digital cameras. The Hubble Space Telescope's Wide Field and Planetary Camera 2 has four ccds; each contains 640,000 pixels. The light collected by each pixel is translated into a number. These numbers (all 2,560,000 of them) are sent to ground-based computers, which convert them into an image.

Charged particles : electrons, protons, ions.

Chasma : Canyon.

Chemical Evolution : The chemical (i.e., pre-biological) changes that transformed simple atoms and molecules into the more complex chemicals needed for the origin of life. For example, hydrogen atoms in the cores of stars combine through nuclear fusion to form the heavier element helium.

Chromosphere : The layer of the solar atmosphere above the PHOTOSPHERE and Beneath the transition region and the CORONA.

A layer of the Sun's atmosphere lying above the photosphere with a width of about 2000 km. It has a lower gas density than the photosphere but a higher temperature. (In fact the temperature continues to rise with altitude, into the corona lying above the chromosphere.) The temperature is sufficiently high to ionize hydrogen gas and produce emission lines, notably the red Balmer line that gives the chromosphere a pinkish color (hence the name, chromo= "color").

The middle layer of the solar atmosphere between the photosphere and the corona. The chromosphere is roughly 10,000 kilometers (6,200 miles) thick and is composed primarily of hydrogen. It varies in temperature from below 10,000 Kelvin (18,000° F) to over 100,000 Kelvin (180,000° F).

Chromospheric events. Some flares are just Chromospheric Events Without Centimetric Bursts or Ionospheric Effects. (SID) (Class C flare)

Cinder cone : A conical hill formed by the accumulation of pyroclastic fragments that fall to the ground in an essentially solid condition.

Cinders : Loose, vesicular volcanic ejecta 4 to 32 millimeters (.16 to 1.28 inches) in diameter.

Circuit Switched Public Data Network (CSPDN) : A type of exchange based telephone system specially designed for the transfer of data.

Clast : A fragment of rock that has been transported, either by volcanic or sedimentary processes.

Clock : A kind of clock, a chip that puts out pulses at regular intervals, controls the basic rhythm of a processor; it keeps the system's activities in step. Its frequency is millions of cycles per second (megahertz, MHz). Eight-bit microcomputers usually have a clock frequency in the range 1 to 8 MHz.

Closed Universe : A geometric model of the universe in which the overall structure of the universe closes upon itself like the surface of a sphere. The rules of geometry in a closed universe are like those that would apply on the surface of a sphere.

A model of the universe that has spherical geometry (hence is finite in space) and which will eventually stop expanding and recollapse (and hence is finite in time as well).

Closed User Group (CUG) : A group of subscribers to Prestel (for instance) who have access to the public pages but can also send information to each other privately.

Cluster : A star network.

Cluster Controller : A device for handling access to a processor by a number of channels (see also multiplexer).

CNO Cycle : This is another path by which H is fused to form He. It requires carbon to act as a catalyst and is believed to be the chief mechanism in stars of 3 solar masses and higher which contain carbon.

A series of nuclear reactions that convert 4 hydrogen into 1 **helium** nucleus. The process starts with the capture of a proton (hydrogen nucleus) onto Carbon turning it into Nitrogen. Eventually further reactions turn the Nitrogen into an Oxygen, and the process is completed by the ejection of an alpha particle (helium nucleus) and the return to Carbon. Thus, carbon acts as a catalyst - it is neither destroyed nor created but simply facilitates the H —> He process. The CNO cycle is important only in stars more massive than the Sun.

Co-Axial Cable (Co-Ax) : Wire with a sleeve of braided metal screening to prevent interference with the signal it carries, as with the wire that connects a TV aerial to the receiving set.

Code : The process of writing out a computer programme is coding; the chunks of programme that result are code. Thus code generators are simply software generators. Codes are also a way of compressing information so that it takes up less space in a channel or a store.

Collecting Area : The area of a telescope's primary light-collecting mirror. A telescope's light-gathering power rises with an increase in its collecting area.

Colles : A small hill or knob.

Colliding Galaxies : A galactic "car wreck" in which two galaxies pass close enough to gravitationally disrupt each other's shape. The collision rips streamers of stars from the galaxies, fuels an explosion of star birth, and can ultimately result in both galaxies merging into one.

Collisional Process : An event involving a collision of objects; for example, the excitation of a hydrogen atom when it is hit by an electron.

Color : The visual perception of light that enables human eyes to differentiate between wavelengths of the visible spectrum, with the longest wavelengths appearing red and the shortest appearing blue or violet.

Color Index : The difference in a star's brightness (magnitude) as measured in two different wavelength bands. For example, suppose one of the two bands were centered on red and the other on blue. Suppose blue was larger: taking the difference of blue minus red brightness would give you a number that quickly shows that the star is blue. Since color indices are measured in units of magnitudes their use can be somewhat confusing since the larger the magnitude the fainter the brightness.

COM : Computer output to microform.

Coma : A hazy cloud which surrounds the nucleus of a comet. A comet's atmosphere (composed of dust and/or various gases) surrounding its nucleus. The coma is rather tenuous (except very close to the nucleus), and stars can be occasionally easily seen through it, shining from behind. And yet, the coma is usually thick enough that it masks our view of the true nucleus of the comet, as seen from the earth. As a comet's nucleus is usually quite small, it is not able to retain its coma for long periods of time, and the coma material gradually drifts away into space (helped out by the solar wind). Much coma material is thrown back into what we see as the comet's tail. But all coma material originates in the comet's nucleus, and solar sublimation due to heating causes gases to move outward, often in jets, taking dust material with them to form the coma and tail.

Comet : A medium-sized icy object orbiting the Sun; smaller than a planet

A comet is a planetesimal in orbit around the sun. Comets are believed to be composed of dust and volatile ices. When close to the sun, comets become heated enough to produce a coma of gas and dust. As this gas and dust moves outward from the comet, it is "blown" away by the solar wind and forms the comet's tail.

A ball of rock and ice, often referred to as a "dirty snowball." Typically a few kilometers in diameter, comets orbit the Sun in paths that either allow them to pass by the Sun only once or that repeatedly bring them through the solar system (as in the 76-year orbit of Halley's Comet). A comet's "signature" long, glowing tail is formed when the Sun's heat warms the coma or nucleus, which releases vapors into space.

A celestial body orbiting the sun (though some may be ejected from the solar system by planetary perturbations) that displays (at least during a portion of its orbit) some diffuseness and/or a "tail" of debris that points generally in the anti-solar direction. Both the diffuseness (generally called a coma) and the tail are composed of gas and/or dust of various atomic or molecular compositions, as is ascertained by spectroscopy. The coma and tail material come from a much smaller nucleus that is usually invisible due to the bright surrounding coma activity. Close-up pictures of a cometary nucleus did not occur until spacecraft fly-bys of Halley's comet in 1986. A more detailed explanation of what a comet is may be found in the Press Information Sheet on comet C/1995 O1 (Hale-Bopp).

A diffuse body of solid particles and gas, which orbits the Sun. The orbit is usually highly elliptical or even parabolic. Comets are unstable bodies with masses of the order of 10^18 g whose average lifetime is about 100 perihelion passages. Periodic comets comprise only ~4% of all known comets. Periodic comets are designated by a number, followed by "P/" and its name. E.g. Halley's comet has the designation 1P/Halley, the parent body of the Perseids, 109P/Swift-Tuttle.

Comet Shoemaker-Levy 9 (SL-9) : A comet that became gravitationally bound to Jupiter, colliding with the planet in July 1994. Prior to entering the planet's atmosphere, the comet broke into several distinct pieces, each with a separate coma and tail.

Command Mode : A style of system use in which the user controls the action by typing in commands (direct instructions) or command codes, instead of choosing options from a menu.

Common Carrier : A provider of basic telecommunications facilities who takes no particular responsibility for the uses to which it is put.

Communications Software : Programmes that enable a computer user to transfer messages and data files over a distance, often using a telephone link, perhaps with features like autodialling and help menus.

Compact Disc (CD) : A 12 cm disc, designed to store high quality audio signals; also able to carry hundreds of megabytes of digital data, leading to CD-ROM, a method for putting very large amounts of data online to a computer in read-only form. Another field is CD-I (compact disc interactive), an approach rather like that of interactive video.

Compact Radio Source : An object emitting radio wavelength emission from a small unresolved region. An example would be the very core of a radio galaxy.

Compatibility : This rare quality in the world of electronic equipment is almost unheard of among microcomputers: even when people describe two systems as compatible, it may not necessarily mean that programmes or data can be taken from one and fed straight to the other.

Compiler : A computer programme that translates an instruction in a high level language like Basic into machine code, done as a once-and-for-all job, unlike an interpreter.

Composite volcano : A volcano composed of interbedded lava and pyroclastic material commonly with steep slopes.

Comprehensive Care : A way of providing health care in which a team of professionals works with the patient to improve his or her physical, emotional, and mental well-being.

Comprehensive Flare Index (CFI) : The indicative of solar flare importance Given by the sum of the following five components A) Importance of ionizing radiation as indicated by time- Associated Short Wave Fade or Sudden Ionospheric Disturbance; (Scale 0-3) B) Importance of H-Alpha flare; (Scale 0-3) C) Magnitude of 10cm flux; (Characteristic of log of flux in units Of 10**-22Watt/m**2/Hz) D) Dynamic spectrum; (Type II = 1, Continuum = 2, Type IV with Duration > 10 minutes = 3) E) Magnitude of 200mhz flux; (Characteristic of log of flux in Units of 10**-22Watt/m**2/Hz)

Compression : Cutting down the space needed to store, or the signal needed to carry, a given package of data (such as a video frame or an electronic mail message), various techniques being in use.

Pressing or squeezing together; done to slow and stop bleeding.

Compton Gamma-Ray Observatory (CGRO) **:** A space-based observatory that collected high-energy gamma-ray light from celestial objects. The Compton satellite consisted of the BATSE, COMPTEL, EGRET, and OSSE instruments. Astronauts aboard the space shuttle Atlantis deployed the CGRO into low-Earth orbit in April 1991. The satellite plunged into the Pacific Ocean in June 2000.

Computer Output to Microform (COM) : A process in which microfiches or film are produced as direct computer output rather than having to be photographed from printout.

Computer-Aided Design (CAD) : Software packages that help design work by giving good graphics, a library of standard sub-designs, modelling, analysis, and simulation.

Computer-Aided Manufacture (CAM) : The digital control of machine tools and assembly lines in an integrated manner.

Concentrator : A modern form of multiplexer with its own processing power.

Concept Keyboard : An input device of value to users who find a standard keyboard an obstacle. Instead of having to type out words letter by letter, the user presses the part of the surface that bears a picture or symbol representing a particular concept. The board accepts a variety of overlays, so can be adapted to different software.

Concurrent : Literally means occurring at the same time. Multi-tasking is a technique for making a number of programmes seem to run in parallel, by letting them take turns at the processor. Concurrent cp/m is a version of the cp/m operating system designed for this purpose. In *true* concurrent processing, a number of processors linked together in parallel (as in a transputer) can really do different things at the same time.

Conduction : Conduction is a process of heat transport through the physical collisions of the particles making up a substance. Similar to electrical conductivity, substances have heat conductivity. Substances with large heat conductivity can transfer heat rapidly (e.g. A hot metal plate). Some substances have low conductivity; they are insulators (e.g., an insulating blanket of foam). Conductivity is an important heat transfer mechanism within white dwarf stars, but not in stars such as the Sun.

Conference Call : A telephone call in which more than two people participate.

Configuration : A particular configuration, or combination of equipment and software, makes up a working system. To configure a system is to modify it to meet some individual set of needs.

Confravision : British Telecom's public video-conferencing system.

Conjugate points : Two points on the earth's surface, at opposite ends of a Geomagnetic field line.

Conjunction : An inferior planet is said to be "in inferior conjunction" when it is directly between the Earth and the Sun. It is "in superior conjunction" when it is on the opposite side of the Sun from the Earth. A superior planet is "in conjunction" when it is on the opposite side of the Sun from the Earth. A superior planet obviously cannot have an inferior conjunction. When the Earth is at inferior conjunction with respect to an observer on a superior planet we say that planet is "in opposition" from Earth's perspective.

The point where an object in our solar system (usually a planet) is the farthest from Earth. The sun will be between Earth and the object, so the object will be visible in the early morning or early evening skies. In the case of the two inner planets (Mercury and Venus), there is an **Inferior Conjunction**, which is when the planet passes directly between Earth and the Sun.

Conservation of Energy And Mass **:** A fundamental law of physics, which states that the total amount of mass and energy in the universe remains unchanged. However, mass can be converted to energy, and vice versa.

Console : The main terminal in a large system, for use by the chief operator, though the term sometimes loosely means any workstation.

Constellation : A geometric pattern of bright stars that appears grouped in the sky. Ancient observers named many constellations after gods, heroes, animals, and mythological beings. Leo (the Lion) is one example of the 88 constellations.

Consultant : An expert (in theory) in some aspect of IT, with (in theory) no ties to any particular system or supplier, and therefore able to give (in theory) valid impartial aid and advice to a user.

Consumables : Anything you need a regular supply of, like printer paper and fuses.

Contact Binary : Two stars in a binary system that are so close together that they share a common envelope of gas. There gravitational fields overlap and the stars form a "peanut" shaped object, like a double-cored, "figure 8" object.

Continuity of mass : In calculating models for stars, it is often convenient to think of them as being composed of many layers like an onion. Continuity of mass implies that at any of these layers, the mass interior to the layer is equal to the sum of the masses of the individual layers inside.

Continuous Infusion : The use of factor concentrates in an ongoing infusion to maintain a steady level of factor within a patient's bloodstream.

Continuous Spectrum : A smooth spectrum of emitted light with all wavelengths present overs some broad range of wavelengths. Blackbodies give off continuous spectra. The rainbow of colors seen when sunlight passes through a prism is an example of a continuous spectrum. In contrast, if some discrete lines are missing one is observing an absorption spectrum. If only discrete lines are present one is observing an emission spectrum.

Continuous Stationery : Paper supplied in continuos form, e.g. fanfold, as opposed to separate sheets.

Continuum storm (ctm) : General term for solar noise lasting for hours and Sometimes days.

Control Codes : Used to make screens and printers produce a variety of effects, like colour, margins, bold face and underlining.

Control Programme : Operating software.

Convection : Convection carries energy by physically moving the hot material up through the gas until it is able to radiate that energy and sink back again. "Convective zones" exist in stars wherever and whenever photons are not able to carry the energy efficiently enough. A process of heat transfer in which hot material physically moves from a hot region to a cooler region (and cool material moves into the hot region). An example of convection is boiling where hot water, heated from below, rises to the surface to cool, while cooler surface water sinks to the bottom to be heated. The cycle continues with a net transport of heat from the bottom to the top. Convection is an important mechanism for heat transport within some types of stars and within certain regions of other types of stars. In the Sun convection is important in the top layers.

Convection Zone : The region below a star's surface where energy flows outward by the rising of hot gas known as convection.

Convergence : Describes technologies that were previously separate but are now coming together and making use of the same basic principles (e.g. digital coding of information) and sometimes even the same equipment (like video receiver-monitors and compact disc or video disc players).

Coordinated Universal Time. By international agreement, the local time at The prime meridian, which passes through Greenwich, England. Therefore, it is also known as GREENWICH MEAN TIME, or sometimes Simply UNIVERSAL TIME.

Copernicus, Nicolaus 1473-1543 : Polish astronomer who advanced the heliocentric theory that the Earth and other planets revolve around the Sun. This was highly controversial at the time as the Ptolemaic view of the universe, which was the prevailing theory for over 1000 years, was deeply ingrained in the prevailing philosophy and religion. (It should be noted, however, that the heliocentric idea was first put forth by Aristarcus of Samos in the 3rd century BC, a fact known to Copernicus but long ignored).

Coping : What a person does in order to avoid, remove, minimize, or get through a stressful situation.

Core : The central part of an object; the core of a planet is the center of the planet

The center region of a star where the temperature, pressure and density are the highest. In main sequence stars the core is where nuclear reactions take place. White dwarf stars are the left over cores of stars that have ejected their outer layers.

Core Collapse : Catastrophic gravitational infall of the center of a star when it no longer can generate sufficient pressure to maintain hydrostatic equilibrium.

Corona : The upper level of the solar atmosphere, characterized by low densities and high temperatures (> 1.0E+06 K); it is not visible from the Earth except during a total eclipse of the sun or by use of special telescopes called coronagraphs.

An ovoid-shaped feature.

The atmosphere of the Sun composed of hot, very thin gas, extending out away from the Sun for a substantial distance. This gas emits light but normally that light can't be seen against the direct glare of the Sun. During a total eclipse this direct light is blocked by the moon and the ghostly white glow of the corona becomes visible.

The outermost layer of the atmosphere of a star, including the Sun. The corona is visible during a solar eclipse or when special adapters or filters are attached to a telescope to block the light from the star's central region. The gaseous corona extends millions of kilometers from the star's surface and has a temperature in the millions of degrees.

Coronagraph : A special telescope which blocks light from the disk of the Sun in order to study the faint solar atmosphere.

Coronal Hole : An extended region of the CORONA, exceptionally low in density And associated with unipolar photospheric regions.

Regions in the corona from which the high-speed solar wind is known to originate. Coronal holes, usually found near the Sun's poles, are large regions in the corona that are less dense and cooler than the surrounding region.

Coronal Mass Ejection : The ejection of a large amount of material from the Sun. Also refered to as a CME. *"As if the Sun lets loose a big burp!" - Dr. P. Erickson*

Coronal Rain (crn) : Material condensing in the CORONA and appearing to rainDown into the CHROMOSPHERE as observed in H-ALPHA at the solar LIMB Above strong SUNSPOTS.

Coronal transients : A general term for short-time-scale changes in the CORONA, but principally used to describe outward-moving PLASMA Clouds.

Corporate Communication : Meeting the information needs within a firm or group, such as by putting up notices, sending out circulars or a house magazine, or publishing the occasional video for the staff.

Corruption : wanted changes to data within a computer system or during transfer over a distance, as a result of software mistakes, interference or attenuation.

Cosmic Abundances : The relative proportions of chemical elements in the Sun, the solar system, and the local region of the Milky

Way galaxy. These proportions are determined by studies of the spectral lines in astronomical objects and are averaged for many stars in our cosmic neighborhood. For example, for every million hydrogen atoms in an average star like our Sun, there are 98,000 helium atoms, 360 carbon atoms, 110 nitrogen atoms, 850 oxygen atoms, and so on.

Cosmic Background Radiation : The blackbody radiation, now mostly in the microwave band, which consists of relic photons left over from the very hot, early phase of the Big Bang.

Cosmic Microwave Background : Radiative energy filling the universe that is believed to be the radiation remaining from the Big Bang. It is sometimes called the "primal glow." This radiation is strongest in the microwave part of the spectrum but has also been detected at radio and infrared wavelengths. The intensity of the cosmic microwave background from every part of the sky is almost exactly the same.

Cosmic Ray : An extremely energetic (relativistic) charged particle.

Electromagnetic rays of extremely high frequency and energy; cosmic rays usually interact with the atoms of the atmosphere before reaching the surface of the Earth. Some cosmic rays come from outside the solar system while others are emitted from the Sun and pass through holes in the corona.

Cosmic rays are very high energy atomic nuclei (mostly protons) traveling through space at high speeds close to that of light. When they hit atoms in the upper atmosphere of the Earth they generate short-lived exotic particles, in much the same way that experimental particle accelerators like CERN or Fermilab work.

High-energy atomic particles that travel through space at speeds close to the speed of light; also known as cosmic-ray particles.

Cosmological : Having to do with the study of the history, structure, and changes in the Universe.

Cosmological Principle : The principle that there is no center to the universe, that the universe is the same in all directions and the same everywhere, when considered on the largest scales. This principle means that what we observe of the universe from our specific location will be representative of the true nature of the universe.

This principle states that the distribution of matter across very large distances is the same everywhere in the universe and that the universe looks the same in all directions. According to this principle, our view of the universe is like the view from a boat on an ocean, which is essentially the same for any other person on any other boat on any other ocean. Measurements of matter and energy in the universe on the largest observable scales support the cosmological principle.

Cosmology : The investigation of the origin, structure, and development of the universe, including how energy, forces, and matter interact on a cosmic scale.

The study of the history, structure and dynamics of the Universe. Cosmologists study how the Universe might have formed, why galaxies are where they are today, and the ultimate fate of the Universe. For more on cosmology check out this primer.

Cosmonaut : An astronaut from the former Soviet Union or the current republic of Russia.

CP/M : The nearest thing to a standard operating system for eight-bit microcomputers, always known by its initials; you can think of it as 'control programme for microprocessors'. There are also 16-bit and network versions.

CPA : Critical path analysis.

CPI :characters per inch, used to measure printer typefaces.

CPS : Characters per second, used to measure printer speed.

CPU : Processor.

Crash : When a programme stops before the end, we say it has crashed. Good software design should prevent this, and may then be called crash-proof. A head crash is when the read/write head of a drive touches a disc surface and causes damage and loss of data.

Crater : A depression formed by the impact of a meteorite.

A depression around the orifice of a volcano.

A bowl-shaped depression caused by a comet or meteorite colliding with the surface of a planet, moon, or asteroid. On geologically active moons and planets (like Earth), craters can result from volcanic activity.

Cratons : The relatively stable portions of continents composed of shield areas and platform sediments; typically, cratons are bounded by tectonically active regions characterized by uplift, faulting and volcanic activity.

Cretaceous period : A geological term denoting the interval of Earth history beginning around 144 million years ago and ending 66 million years ago.

Cretaceous-Tertiary boundary : A major stratigraphic boundry on Earth marking the end of the Mesozoic Era, best known as the age of the dinosaurs. The boundary is defined by a global extinction event that caused the abrupt demise of the majority of all life on Earth.

Critical Density : The minimum average density that matter in the universe would need in order for its gravitational pull to slow the universe's expansion to a halt.

The mass density of the universe which just stops the expansion of space, after infinite cosmic time has elapsed. The critical density is the boundary value between universe models that expand forever (open models) and those that recollapse (closed models). A measurement of the actual density of the universe could be compared to the critical density which would then, in principle, indicate the fate of the cosmos.

Critical Path Analysis (CPA) : A technique, now often used with the aid of a computer, to schedule the tasks involved in, and the resources needed by, a project.

Crochet : A sudden deviation in the sunlit geomagnetic field (H component; See GEOMAGNETIC ELEMENTS) associated with large solar FLARE X-ray emission.

CRT : Cathode ray tube.

Crystalline : Rock types made up of crystals or crystal fragments, such as metamorphic rocks that recrystallized in high temperature or pressure environments, or igneous rocks that formed from cooling of a melt.

CSPDN : Circuit switched public data network.

CUG : Closed user group.

Cursor : A symbol on a screen that shows you where you are, usually a square blob or an underline mark and often flashing.

Cut and Paste : The technique of joining chunks of text and pictures together to make a camera-ready copy of a page for printing, now much aided by desktop publishing software on computers.

❒❒❒

D

D REGION : A daytime layer of the earth's IONOSPHERE approximately 50 to 90 km in altitude.

DAC : Digital to analogue converter.

Daisy Wheel : The print head of a type of letter-quality printer used with micros. The characters that can be printed appear as raised shapes on the ends of the spokes (petals) of the wheel, and the wheel spins to put the right ones in place in turn.

Dark Dust Cloud : A region of interstellar space that contains a rich concentration of gas and dust. Such a cloud is often irregular in shape but sometimes has a well-defined edge. Visible light cannot pass through these clouds, so they obscure the light from stars beyond them.

Dark Matter : Dark matter is any matter in the Universe which does not give off any light of its own, or does not interact with light the way typical matter does.

Matter that is too dim to be detected by telescopes. Astronomers infer its existence by measuring its gravitational influence. Dark matter makes up most of the total mass of the universe.3. Term used to describe any astronomical mass that does not produce significant light and hence is hard to observe. Examples of dark matter include planets, black holes, white dwarfs (because they are low luminosity) and more exotic things like weakly interacting particles (wimps).

Dark nebulae : Although not initially recognized by astronomers, it is clear now that interstellar dust often occurs in substantial clouds which obscure the light coming from behind them. These are referred to as dark nebulae.

d'**Arrest, Heinrich Louis :** Danish astronomer who assisted Galle with the first observations of Neptune. After receiving its predicted position from Le Verrier, Galle and d'Arrest began searching.

With Galle at the eyepiece and d'Arrest reading the chart, they scanned the sky and checked that each star seen was actually on the chart. Just a few minutes after their search began, d'Arrest cried out, "That star is not on the map!" and earned his place in the history books.

DAT : Digital audio tape.

Data : Generally, information without meaning, even if in the form of letters or numbers that you can read. Sometimes people restrict it to mean information after a system has prepared it for processing or transfer.

Data Capture : The process by which a computer automatically obtains data from its environment or the process by which people obtain information so that it can be fed into a computer with few errors.

Data Haven : A country where there are no restrictions on the processing, exchange and sale of data. Countries with data protection laws may restrict the export of data since their laws could be evaded so easily in data havens.

Data Processing (DP) : Loosely, the handling of information, this usually refers in practice to the batch processing by computer of large volumes of prepared data, such as telephone bills or a payroll.

Data Protection : Procedures and laws designed to ensure the privacy and security of stored personal data.

Data Skew : When data pass through a parallel link over a long distance, bits that set off together do not always arrive exactly together. This lack of alignment is skew.

Data Subject : Anyone on whom information is stored.

Databank : A collection – usually a large one – of data held in a computer, the term sometimes being used interchangeably with database.

Database (DB) : A collection of information files organized systematically so as to make processing easy. Database management systems (DBMS) are computer programmes for designing a database, and allowing its use, normally by more than one person.

Datafax : A public fax system.

DB : Database.

DBMS : Database management system (see database).

DBS : Direct broadcast (by) satellite.

Debug : To remove mistakes (bugs).

Decaying orbit : A path around an object which decreases in size with time. For example, when a satellite enters a decaying orbit above Earth, its orbit size decreases to the point that it enters Earth's atmosphere where it burns up.

Declination : Declination is the angular distance on the celestial sphere north or south of the celestial equator. It is measured along the hour circle passing through the celestial object.

One of two celestial coordinates required to locate an astronomical object, such as a star, on the celestial sphere. Declination is the measure of angular distance of a celestial object above or below the celestial equator and is comparable to latitude. To familiarize yourself with declination, hold out your arm in the direction of the North Star (Polaris). You are now pointing at plus 90 degrees declination. Move your arm downward by 90 degrees. You are now pointing at 0 degrees declination.

A coordinate used on the celestial sphere just as latitude is used on Earth. An object's declination is measured in degrees from the celestial equator; positive degrees if north of the equator, and negative if south of the equator. Also see right ascension.

Celestial coordinate system used to measure latitude above or below the celestial equator on the celestial sphere.

One element of the astronomical coordinate system on the sky that is used by astronomers. Declination, which can be thought of as latitude on the earth projected onto the sky, is usually denoted by the lower-case Greek letter delta and is measured north (+) and south (-) of the celestial equator in degrees, minutes, and seconds of arc. The celestial equator is defined as being at declination zero (0) degrees; the north and south celestial poles are defined as being at +90 and -90 degrees, respectively. When specifying a comet's location on the sky, one must state the right ascension and declination (with equinox), along with date and time (since a comet moves with respect to the background stars). For examples of how right ascension (R.A.) and declination (Decl.)

Dedicated : Specially designed for, or limited to, a particular purpose, as opposed to being programmeable.

Default : The value or behaviour that a system assumes unless otherwise instructed.

Degree : A unit used in the measurement of angles, heavily used particularly in astronomy. Due to ancient Babylonian mathematics, we still divide a circle into 360 even units of arc and call each of these units one degree. The entire sky, therefore, spans 360 degrees. Up to about 180 degrees of sky is visible from any given point on earth with an unobstructed horizon (as measured from, say, east to west, or north to south). The degree is used to make measurements of distance, or position (as with declination) in astronomy. In turn, a degree is composed of 60 minutes of arc, and also of 360 seconds of arc.

Degree of Arc : One degree of arc is 1/360 of a full circle. The apparent sizes of objects as seen from Earth can be measured in degrees of arc. The angular diameter of the full moon or the Sun as seen from Earth is one-half of a degree.

Delta : The upper-case Greek letter used to denote an object's geocentric distance in ephemeris tables; see "ephemeris". (Note that lower-case delta is used to denote declination.)

Demodulator : A device that reconstructs an original signal from a modulated version, e.g. digital computer data from the analogue version received through a telephone system (see modem).

Density : Measured in grams per cubic centimeter (or kilograms per liter); the density of water is 1.0; iron is 7.9; lead is 11.3.

The density of an object is equal to the mass of that object divided by its volume. Substances (like lead, water, iron, granite) have a certain density under normal pressures. In such cases the density of a substance can also be used to determine how much mass will be present given a certain volume of the substance. For example, water has a density of 1 gram per cubic centimeter (gm/cm^3) so a cube of water 10 centimeters on a side weighs 1000 gm (1 kilogram). Some substances (like gases) are compressible and have different densities depending on how much pressure is exerted upon them. The Sun is composed of compressible (and hot!) Gases and is much denser at its center than near its surface.

The mass per unit of volume of a substance.

The ratio of the mass of an object to its volume. For example, water has a density of one gram of mass for every milliliter of volume. Depressed northward field component returns to normal levels.

Desensitization : Repeated exposure to medical experiences, equipment, and procedures through books, films, and medical play. This process helps reduce children's fears and anxieties associated with medical experiences and helps them gain a sense of control and familiarity.

Desktop Publishing (DTP) : With desktop publishing software a compact in-house computer system is used to produce pages of professionally laid-out text and graphics ready for printing.

Detached Binary : An "ordinary" binary star system where the two stars are well separated from each other. Each star evolves on its own, in a manner similar to an isolated star.

Deuterium : A special form of hydrogen (an isotope called "heavy hydrogen") that has a neutron as well as a proton in its nucleus.

Dialect : A variant of a programming language, e.g. Basic exists in hundreds of different dialects, all incompatible to some extent.

Dialogue : An exchange of questions and answers between a computer programme and a user.

Diameter : The distance from one side to the other through the center of a circle or a sphere, such as a planet

Diaplectic Glass : A natural glass formed by shock pressure from any of several minerals without melting; it is found only in association with meteorite impact craters.

Dielectric Constant : The ratio of electric flux density to electric field.

Differential Rotation : The change in SOLAR ROTATION RATE with latitude. Low Latitudes rotate at a faster angular rate (approx. 14 degrees per Day) than do high latitudes (approx. 12 degrees per day).

Differentiation : The separation of heavy matter from light matter, thus causing a variation in density and composition. Differentiation occurs in an object like a planet as gravity draws heavier material toward the planet's center and lighter material rises to the surface.

Diffraction Grating : A device that splits light into its component parts or spectrum. A diffraction grating often consists of a mirror with thousands of closely spaced parallel lines, which spread out the light into parallel bands of colors or distinct fine lines or bars.

Digital : Anything that can be counted as separate numbers, the opposite of analog – a digital signal is step-like, while an analog one is wavy.

Digital Audio Tape (DAT) : Magnetic tape on which analog sound signals can be stored in digital form, and therefore with very high quality and potential for computer backing store.

Digital Image : A visible image that is recorded by an electronic detector and subdivided into small picture elements (pixels). Each element is assigned a number that corresponds to the brightness recorded at its physical location on the detector. Computer software converts the numerical information into a visual image. The Hubble Space Telescope records digital images.

Digital Optical Disc (DOD) : A video disc that carries its data in digital rather than analog form, so has potential in computer backing storage.

Digital to Analog Converter (DAC) : A device that changes digital information into analog form e.g. it may allow the output of a digital computer to control analog devices like motors and transfer to traditional telephone systems.

Digital Voice Messaging : The speech equivalent of store and forward electronic mail, voice messages being held by the host computer in digital form.

Digitizer : Any device able to give a digital output from some form of analog input. The term is most often used for graphics pads, for scanners, and for systems that capture a video signal so that it can be processed by computer.

Dinosaurs : Large animals that lived in the Mesozoic Era from 230 to 65 million years ago; most probably wiped out by the impact of a large asteroid or comet.

Direct : Rotation or orbital motion in a counterclockwise direction when viewed looking down from above the north pole of the primary (i.e. In the same sense to most satellites); the opposite of retrograde. The north pole is the one on the same side of the ecliptic as the Earth's north pole. (The word "prograde" is sometimes used to mean "direct" in this sense.)

Direct Access : Also (less wisely) called random access, this describes how any part of a computer memory, back-up disc or video disc can be found quickly without having to work through from the start The opposite of serial access (as in a cassette that has to be wound through from the beginning).

Direct Broadcast by Satellite (DBS) : Using a satellite to relay the signals sent to it so that they can be picked up in a large area by anyone with a suitable aerial.

Direct Connect Modem : A modem that connects directly to the telephone network, unlike all acoustic coupler.

Directory : Catalogue.

Disable : To prevent from operating; sometimes it is useful to disable a key (like a computer's <BREAK> key, pushing which may wipe out a programme) or a device (e.g. a printer, if printout is not needed). The opposite of enable.

Disappearing solar filament (DSF) : The sudden (timescale of minutes toHours) disappearance of a solar FILAMENT (PROMINENCE).

Disaster : Literally "bad stars"; particularly apt in reference to a major asteroid impact.

Disc : A flat circular sheet of material used to store information (US, disk). It may be hard (rigid) or flexible (floppy). Discs for computer data storage are magnetic, compact and video discs are non-magnetic.

Disc Drive : A device that retrieves (reads) information from and records (writes) it to a disc, working with discs only of suitable type, size, density and number of tracks.

Disc Operating System (DOS) : A computer programme that controls the storage and access of data on discs.

Disc Pack : A stack of hard (rigid) magnetic discs.

Disk : The visible surface of the Sun (or any heavenly body) projected against the sky.

Disk, Galactic : The flattened, rotating portion of the Galaxy, centered on the galactic nucleus, containing much dust and gas as well as newly formed stars. Galactic disks are found in sprial galaxies and often exhibit prominent spiral arms.

Diskette : A floppy disc, a term mainly found in the US.

Distance Ladder : The series of techniques employed by astronomers to obtain distances to progressively more distant astronomical objects.

Distance Modulus : The formula for obtaining the distance to a star using the difference between the absolute and apparent magnitude of a star, (m-M). The formula is (m-M) = 5 log(d/10), where d is the distance as measured in parsecs. If a star has a distance modulus of m-M = 0 then it is exactly 10 pc away because the apparent and absolute magnitudes are equal. A positive value of the distance modulus means the apparent magnitude is larger than the absolute, i.e., the star is fainter than it would appear at a distance of 10 pc.

Distributed Database : Has its banks of data shared between several computer systems. Sometimes used to describe an electronically published database.

Distributed Processing : The generic phrase for using either intelligent terminals with a mainframe or mini, or a network system.

Diurnal Path : The apparent daily path of the Sun in the sky. See celestial sphere for a helpful diagram.

Diversion : Used to increase the child's cooperation with what is needed to complete a medical experience or procedure without risking a loss of the child's trust in you. This non-invasive technique can help alter the perception of pain by diverting the mind to a more pleasurable experience.

Documentation : Printed instructions and manuals that are vital if a user is to get the best out of any system; an important (but often neglected) part of a package.

Dog Star : Another name for Sirius, the brightest star visible in the night sky.

Dongle : A cartridge containing a chip that you must plug in to a computer before you can work with the software – it thus protects against illicit use.

Doppler effect - Apparent change in wavelength of the radiation from a source due to its relative motion away from or towards the observer.

(Christian Doppler 1803-1853) the apparent change in wavelength of sound or light caused by the motion of the source, observer or both. (see also)

The change in the wavelength of sound or light waves caused when the object emitting the waves moves toward or away from the observer; also called Doppler Shift. In sound, the Doppler Effect causes a shift in sound frequency or pitch (for example, the change in pitch noted as an ambulance passes). In light, an object's visible color is altered and its spectrum is shifted toward the blue region of the spectrum for objects moving toward the observer and toward the red for objects moving away.

When a source of light (or sound) is moving towards or away from an observer (radial velocity) the photons (or sound waves) show a shift in wavelength from what would be observed for a stationary source. The ratio of the magnitude of the shift to the rest wavelength is equal to the ratio of the radial velocity to the velocity of light (or sound). The sense of the shift is towards longer wavelengths (redshift) for receding objects and shorter wavelengths for objects coming towards us. This effect is observed in many situations in astronomy and enables us to measure such things as the temperature of stellar atmospheres, stellar atmospheric turbulence, stellar rotation, binary star motions for spectroscopic binaries, individual motions of stars and galaxies relative to the Sun, and the rotation of galaxies.

Doppler shift : A shift in an object's spectrum due to a change in the wavelength of light that occurs when an object is moving toward or away from Earth.

The change in frequency of a wave (light, sound, etc.) Due to the relative motion of source and receiver. Things moving toward you have their wavelengths shortened. Things moving away have their emitted wavelengths lengthened.

Dorsum : A ridge.

DOS : Disc operating system.

Dot Matrix : Describes a printer that forms characters from a matrix (grid) of dots, the more dots possible, the better the shape of the character.

Download : Transfer of data from one computer to a smaller one, typically from a mainframe to a terminal or from a network to a workstation.

Downward Compatible : Able to work with hardware or software that is simpler or older.

DP : Data processing: large firms often have separate DP departments with DP managers in charge.

Dramatic Play : Expression and release of fears, frustration, tension, and anger through play-acting.

Drexon : Drexon film is able to carry digital data at high density so that a laser can read it for input to a computer system. Its uses are on video discs, tapes and cards.

Dst INDEX : A geomagnetic index describing variations in the equatorial Ringcurrent.

DTP : Desktop publishing.

Dual Sound : With two independent sound tracks, so that the same video material can be viewed with a choice of sound track (perhaps in different languages or aimed at different levels of audience), or the second sound track can be used to provide stereo output.

Dumb : The opposite of intelligent; describes a device with no processing power of its own.

Dump : To copy a block of computer memory somewhere else, e.g. to a printer (thus a screen dump is a printout version of the screen display) or to backing store.

Dust : Tiny grains of stuff, e.g., carbon grains (soot) and silicate grains (sand) that are about 0.1-1.0 micron in size. Dust grains are a major component of the interstellar medium. Dust blocks visible light causing interstellar extinction. Dust scatters incident starlight, particularly the blue wavelengths of light (blue light has a wavelength comparable to the dust grain's size) causing interstellar reddening. The dust itself is cold, and cools even further by giving off infrared emission. Dutch physicist and astronomer who first described the nature of Saturn's rings (1655) and discovered its moon Titan; also pioneered the use of the pendulum in clocks.

Dwarf Galaxy : A relatively small galaxy. The Large and Small Magellanic Clouds, visible in the Southern Hemisphere, are two dwarf irregular galaxies that are neighbors of the Milky Way.

A very faint galaxy. Dwarf galaxies are either small or just not very bright, or sometimes both.

❒❒❒

E

E Region : A daytime layer of the earth's ionosphere roughly between theAltitudes of 85 and 140 km.

E=mc² : Einstein's famous theory of relativity formula known as the energy-mass relation. The energy ***e*** is equal to the mass ***m*** multiplied by the speed of light squared c^2. A small mass produces an enormous amount of energy.

Earth : Orbiting the Sun at a distance of 150 million km, one AU, Earth is a terrcstrial planet, and home to us all.

The third planet from the Sun and one of four terrestrial planets in the inner solar system. Earth, the only planet where water exists in large quantities, has an atmosphere capable of supporting myriad life forms. The planet is 150 million kilometers (93 million miles) away from the Sun. Earth has one satellite — the Moon.

Eccentric : Noncircular; elliptical (applied to an orbit).

Eccentricity : An orbital parameter describing the eccentricity of the orbit ellipse. Eccentricity e is the ratio of half the distance between the foci c to the semi-major axis a: $e=c/a$. For example, an orbit with $e=0$ is circular, $e=1$ is parabolic, and e between 0 and 1 is elliptic.

A value that defines the shape of an ellipse or planetary orbit; the ratio of the distance between the foci and the major axis.

The eccentricity of an ellipse (planetary orbit) is the ratio of the distance between the foci and the major axis. Equivalently the eccentricity is (ra-rp)/(ra+rp) where ra is the apoapsis distance and rp is the periapsis distance.

Eclipse (Lunar) : When the Earth passes directly between the Sun and the Moon, the Earth's shadow will obscure all or part of the lunar surface. Lunar eclipses can only occur during a full moon (when the half of the moon visible to Earth is lit by the Sun).

Eclipse (Solar) : When the Moon passes directly between the Sun and the Earth, the Moon's shadow will obscure all or part of the Sun. Solar eclipses can only occur during a new moon (when the unseen half of the Moon is lit by the Sun).

Eclipsing Binary : A binary star system where one star passes in front of the other at some point in their orbits, as we observe the system. This makes the total light from the system seem to vary with time—it is dimmer during eclipse and brighter when the system is out of eclipse. The way that the light changes as a function of time (such a graph of light versus time is known as a "light curve") can give direct information about the size of the stars and the orientation and size of the orbit.

Ecliptic : The apparent path of the sun against the sky background (celestial sphere); formally, the mean plane of the earth's orbit about the sun.

The orbits of the planets are all (more or less) in the same plane called the ecliptic and defined by the plane of the Earth's orbit. Put another way, the ecliptic is the apparent path of the Sun around the sky during the year. See celestial sphere for a helpful diagram.

The plane of Earth's orbit about the Sun

Edit : To improve, cut or rearrange material, such as text, programmes or video tape. An editor is a device or programme to help you do this.

EDS : Electronic document storage.

Effusive eruption : A relative quiet volcanic eruption which puts out basaltic lava that moves at about the speed one walks; the lava is fluid in nature; the eruptions at the Kilauea volcano on the island of Hawaii are effusive

EFT : Electronic funds transfer.

Einstein, Albert 1879-1955 : German-American physicist; developed the Special and General Theories of Relativity which along with Quantum Mechanics is the foundation of modern physics. (See fusion, speed of light).

Ejecta : Material such as glass and fragmented rock thrown out of an impact crater during its formation.

Electromagnetic Force : A fundamental force that governs all interactions among electrical charges and magnetism. Essentially, all charged particles attract oppositely charged particles and repel identically charged particles. Similarly, opposite poles of magnets attract and like magnetic poles repel.

Electromagnetic Radiation : A form of energy that propagates through space as vibrations of electric and magnetic fields; also called radiation or light. All electromagnetic radiation is a form of light.

Electromagnetic spectrum : The entire range of the different types of electromagnetic radiation, or waves. It goes from the very long wave, low frequency, radio waves through infrared waves and visible light waves to the very high frequency and short waves of the gamma-rays and X-rays. Those wavelengths in the visible light range have a specific color associated with them when they pass through a prism. The lower frequency, longer wavelengths produce a red while those with higher frequency, shorter wavelengths produce a violet. Those wavelengths which fall somewhere in between these two points produce the orange, yellow, green, and blue also found in a spectrum.

Electromagnetic Wave : A wave generated by an electromagnetic field. These waves (unlike sound waves) do NOT require a medium to travel through. Go to The Electromagnetic Spectrum (by Georgia State University) for a chart of the electromagnetic spectrum and a wavelength/frequency calculator.

Vibrations of electrical and magnetic energy that travel together between two points. The electromagnetic spectrum is the full range of electromagnetic waves, usually classed by frequency or wavelength.

Electromagnetism : The science dealing with the physical relationship between electricity and magnetism. The principle of an electromagnet, a magnet generated by electrical current flow, is based on this phenomenon.

Electron : A negatively charge elementary particle that typically resides outside the nucleus of an atom but is bound to it by electromagnetic forces. An electron's mass is tiny: 1,836 electrons equals the mass of one proton.

A sub-atomic particle found orbiting the nuclei of an atom. Unlike the proton and Neutron, the electron has a negative charge.

A tiny particle that has a negative charge

An elementary particle (of the type known as a lepton) with a negative charge. One of the components of atoms, the electrons orbit around the nucleus, and the distribution and number of electrons determine the chemical properties of an element.

Electron Degeneracy : According to the Pauli Exclusion Principle, no two identical particles can occupy the same cell in phase space (as defined by the Heisenberg Uncertainty Principle). While two, otherwise identical, electrons can occupy the same cell if they have opposite directions of spin, in practical terms as the material in a star is compressed into a smaller volume under the force of gravity the electrons find that they must move faster than they normally would in order to find cells in phase space to occupy. This condition is referred to as electron degeneracy. It is an important factor in the onset of He burning in stars and in the structure of White Dwarf stars which are virtually entirely electron degenerate.

Electron Degeneracy Pressure : Quantum mechanics restricts the number of electrons that can have low energy. Basically, each electron must occupy its own energy state. When electrons are packed together, as they are in a white dwarf, the number of available low energy states is too small and many electrons are forced into high energy states. These high energy electrons make a significant contribution to the pressure. Because the pressure arises from this quantum mechanical effect, it is insensitive to temperature, *i.e.*, the pressure doesn't go down as the star cools.

Electron Volt (ev) : A unit of energy that is equal to the energy that an electron gains as it moves through a potential difference of one volt. This very small amount of energy is equal to $1.602 * 10^{-19}$ joules. Because an electron volt is so small, engineers and scientists sometimes use the terms mev (mega-million) and gev (giga-billion) electron volts.

Electronic Document Storage (EDS) : Holding copies of documents (pure text or with graphics) in a form that can be accessed by a computer, such as on some kind of disc.

Electronic Funds Transfer (EFT) : The transfer between computers of data that represents sums of money.

Electronic Mail : A method of transfer of information across a distance using cable, telephone lines, broadcast waves or satellites. Confusingly, some people also use the phrase to describe scrolling interactive videotex (viewdata) systems like British Telecom Gold.

Electronic Office : Jargon used to describe an office in which there is much use of new information technology.

Electronic Publishing : Preparing and storing documents (pure text or with graphics) so that other people can access them by computer, e.g. through a communications link.

Electronics : The technology of systems that involve small electric currents.

Electrons : Sub-atomic particles with negative charge that carry electric current in a metal and also make up the beam in a cathode ray tube.

Element : A substance composed of a particular kind of atom. All atoms with the same number of protons (atomic numbers) in the nucleus are examples of the same element and have identical chemical properties. For example, gold (with 79 protons) and iron (with 26 protons) are both elements, but table salt is not because it is made from two different elements: sodium and chlorine. The atoms of a particular element have the same number of protons in the nucleus and exhibit a unique set of chemical properties. There are about 90 naturally occurring elements on Earth.

Elementary Particles : Particles smaller than atoms that are the basic building blocks of the universe. The most prominent examples are photons, electrons, and quarks.

Particles which cannot be broken into smaller pieces. For example, a table can be broken into table legs and the table top, but a table leg cannot be broken into smaller complete pieces. Electrons, quarks, and other elementary particles cannot be broken into smaller pieces because they are the smallest building blocks of nature.

Elevation : The angular distance of an object above the horizon. 0° is on the horizon and 90° is straight up.

Ellipse : A closed curve that is formed from two foci or points in which the sum of the distances from any point on the curve to the two foci is a constant. Johannes Kepler first discovered that the orbits of the planets are ellipses, not circles; he based his discovery on the careful observations of Tycho Brahe.

A special kind of elongated circle. The orbits of the solar system planets form ellipses.

Oval. That the orbits of the planets are ellipses, not circles, was first discovered by Johannes Kepler based on the careful observations by Tycho Brahe.

Elliptical : Shaped like an elongated closed curve.

Elliptical Galaxy : A galaxy classification in the Hubble scheme, ellipticals get their names from their overall shape. The ellipticals are subclassified by their degree of ellipticity as they appear to the observer. E0 types are completely spherical, and E7 types are very elliptical (i.e., elongated). E1 through E7 have increasing degrees of ellipticity. They are smooth and structureless, and contain mainly old Pop. II type stars. Ellipticals range in size from the relatively rare Giant Ellipticals, which can be as big as a Megaparsec across with a trillion stars, to the very common dwarf ellipticals which can be as small as a kiloparsec across with a million stars.

A galaxy that appears spherical or football-shaped. Elliptical galaxies are comprised mostly of old stars and contain very little dust and "cool" gas that can form stars.

Elongation : Angular distance of a celestial object from the sun in the sky. In standard ephemerides, this is usually denoted by the Greek letter epsilon (or by the abbreviation "Elong."). A celestial (usually solar-system) object's "phase angle" is the elongation of the earth from the sun, as would be seen by an observer on that third celestial object.

Emerging flux region (efr) : An area on the sun where new magnetic flux is Erupting.

Emission Line : A bright line in a spectrum caused by emission of light. Each chemical element emits and absorbs radiated energy at specific wavelengths. The collection of emission lines in a spectrum corresponds to the chemical elements contained in a celestial object.

The bright lines seen against a darker background, created when a hot gas emits photons characteristic of the elements of which the gas is composed.

A glowing cloud of hot interstellar gas. The gas is energized by nearby or embedded hot young stars. The gas is mainly hydrogen and the light mainly hydrogen emission, but other elements (e.g. Nitrogen, oxygen) are also present and also give off their own emission lines.

Emission nebulae : This term applies to clouds of interstellar gas which are excited by the radiation (often in the UV) from hot, young, nearby stars. As a result, they emit radiation of their own, often dominated by the red line of Balmer alpha. The term is also applied to the remnants of supernovae such as the Crab nebula.

Emulation : Making one device behave like another.

En echelon fissures : Fissures that are parallel in trend to each other, but offset to either the left or right.

Enable : To make a key or device operate, as opposed to disable.

Encryption : Converting electronic data in to a coded form before storage or transfer to make illicit access harder.

Energy : Energy is usually defined as "the capacity to do work" but just what does that mean? Work is defined in physics as the exertion of a force over some distance, e.g., lifting a rock up against the gravity of the Earth. You probably have a pretty good colloquial grasp of the idea of "work" as something that takes effort. Energy is also something that is "conserved" within a closed system. This means that it is neither created nor destroyed but simply moved about (possibly changing from one form of energy to another). Light is basically a form of energy, one that radiates through space. So the Sun can release nuclear energy, creating light which travels through space to the Earth, where it can be absorbed by, say, a photocell, which in turn permits a motor to run propelling a solar-powered car forward.

Usable heat or power; in physics, it is the capacity of a physical system to perform work.

Enquiry Language : A high level language specially designed for interrogating (asking questions of) a database, in particular that of an expert system.

Enter : To put instructions or information into a computer.

Envelope : The outer, less dense portion of a star, surrounding the hot, dense core. The outer 3/4 or so of the radius of the Sun is considered to be the envelope.

Eolian : Related to wind deposits and associated effects.

Ephemeral : Not permanent, e.g. a computer's RAM is often ephemeral – its contents vanish when you switch off.

Ephemeris : An ephemeris is a tabulation of computed positions and velocities (and/or various derived quantities such as right ascension and declination) of an orbiting body at specific times. The plural form of ephemeris is ephemerides.

Ephemeris (plural: ephemerides) : A table listing specific data of a moving object, as a function of time. Ephemerides usually contain right ascension and declination apparent angle of elongation from the sun (in degrees), and magnitude (brightness) of the object; other quantities frequently included in ephemerides include the objects distances from the sun and earth (in AU), usually given as Roman letter "r" and Greek letter "Delta", respectively; phase angle; and moon phase.

Ephemeris Time (ET) : Determined in principle from the sun's apparent annual motion, ET is the numerical measure of uniform time, which is the independent variable in the gravitational theory of the earth's orbital motion, coming from Simon Newcomb's *Tables of the Sun*. In practice, ET was obtained by comparing observing positions of the Moon with gravitational ephemerides calculated from theories. In 1992, standard (apparent geocentric) ephemerides of comets and minor planets changed from using Ephemeris Time to Terrestrial Dynamical Time (TDT, or TT).

Episodic : Treatment of bleeds as they occur or as necessary.

Eprom : Erasable programmeable read-only memory; a ROM chip which you can load with a programme that you can later erase. Usually erased by shining ultra-violet light through a circular window over the chip. Eproms are a useful way of distributing firmware that is still being developed and refined.

Equilibrium : A balance in the rates of opposing processes, such as emission and absorption of photons, creation and destruction of matter, etc. So that there is no net change.

Equinox : Either of the two points (vernal, autumnal) on the celestial sphere where the ecliptic (which is the apparent path of the sun on the sky) intersects the celestial equator. Due to precession, this point moves over time, so positions of stars in catalogues and on atlases are usually referred to a "mean equator and equinox" of a specified standard epoch.

Erg/sec : = 1e-10 kilowatts.

Ergonomics : The study of the relationship between the design of equipment and systems and the comfort and efficiency of the people who use it.

Erosion : Natural processes that wear or grind away the surface of an object. On Earth, the major agents of erosion are water and wind.

Eruption : The ejection of volcanic materials (lavas, pyroclasts and volcanic gases) onto the surface, either from a central vent, a fissure or a group of fissures.

Eruptive : Solar activity levels with at least one radio event(10cm) and Several chromospheric events per day (Class C Flares)

Eurptive Prominence on Limb (EPL) : A solar PROMINENCE that becomes activa Ted and is seen to ascend from the sun.

Escape Velocity : The minimum velocity required for an object to escape the gravity of a massive object.

he outward velocity required to leave the surface of a body mass M and radius R and escape to infinity (not fall back). The formula for the escape velocity is $(2GM/R)^{1/2}$.

European Space Agency (ESA) : A fifteen-member consortium of European countries for the design, development, and deployment of satellites. The Space Telescope — European Coordinating Facility (ST-ECF) supports the European astronomical community in exploiting the research opportunities provided by the Earth-orbiting Hubble Space Telescope. The ESA members are Austria, Belgium, Denmark, Finland, France, Germany, Ireland, Italy, the Netherlands, Norway, Portugal, Spain, Sweden, Switzerland, and the United Kingdom, with Canada as a cooperating state.

Event Horizon : 1. A boundary dividing space into a region that can be seen from one that cannot. In the case of a black hole, it is that surface surround the region out of which light itself cannot escape. No signal or information from within the event horizon can reach the outside universe. 2. The spherical outer boundary of a black hole. Once matter crosses this threshold, the speed required for it to escape the black hole's gravitational grip is greater than the speed of light.

Evolutionary Track : As a star ages and evolves, its location on the HR diagram changes. If you trace out all the locations of a given star during its lifetime you get an evolutionary track on the HR diagram for that star. Such tracks are a compact and convenient way to show how a star changes over its lifetime.

Exchange : Switching centre in a public telephone network, for instance.

Excitation : When an atom absorbs a photon and is raised to a higher energy level.

Excited State : A greater-than-minimum energy state of any atom that is achieved when at least one of its electrons resides at a greater-than-normal distance from its parent nucleus.

Execute : The stage when a processor actually carries out the instructions in a programme.

Executive : A type of operating software.

Expansion Factor : The amount by which the universe has scaled up in size since an earlier time due to the expansion of space. The scale factor is equal to 1+z where z is the cosmological redshift.

Expert System : The name given to software that builds up expertise in making judgements and displays artificial intelligence. Some expert systems can converse with humans in a relatively natural way, and some can explain and justify their line of 'reasoning'. So far, the most successful expert systems tend to operate in a restricted field of knowledge; these may be called knowledge-based expert systems.

Explosive eruption : A dramatic volcanic eruption which throws debris high into the air for hundreds of miles; lava is low in silicate; can be very dangerous for people near by; an example is Mount St. Helens in 1980

Exponential notation : "1.23e4" means "1.23 times 10 to the fourth power" or 12,300; "5.67e-8" means "5.67 divided by 10 to the eighth power" or 0.0000000567.

Expressive Play : Expression of feelings and energy in acceptable, pleasurable, and physical ways.

Extension : A telephone handset without its own direct line to an exchange.

External Memory : The storage of information outside a computer, usually in magnetic form such as on disc.

Extinction, atmospheric : The diminishing of light from astronomical objects due to the earth's atmosphere, in which molecules (air, dust, etc.) Of the atmosphere absorb, reflect, and refract light before it reaches the ground. Extinction becomes a severe problem for astronomers when objects are viewed close to (especially within 20 degrees of) the local horizon. There are various methods that have been developed for astronomers to try and compensate for this extinction, but it is always best to make measurements of astronomical objects when they are as high in the sky as possible (to minimize errors).

Extraterrestrial : An adjective that means "beyond the Earth." The phrase "extraterrestrial life" refers to possible life on other planets.

Extreme Ultraviolet (EUV) : A portion of the electromagnetic spectrum from Approximately 100 to 1000 angstroms.

Extremely Low Frequency (ELF) : That portion of the radio frequency spectrum From 30 to 3000 hertz.

❑❑❑

F

F Corona : of the white-light CORONA (that is, the corona seen by the eye at A total solar (ECLIPSE), that portion which is caused by sunlight Scattered or reflected by solid particles (dust) in inter-Planetary space.

F Region : The upper layer of the IONOSPHERE, approximately 120 to 1500 km In altitude. The F region is subdivided into the F1 and F2 Regions. The F2 region is the most dense and peaks at altitudes Between 200 and 600 km. The F1 region is a smaller peak in Electron density, which forms at lower altitudes in the daytime.

Facsimile Transfer : Fax.

Factor Concentrates : Purified clotting factor freeze-dried into a convenient powder form.

Facula : Bright spot. A bright region of the PHOTOSPHERE seen in white light, seldom Visible except near the solar LIMB.

Faculae : A bright region of the photosphere seen in white light, seldom visible except near the solar limb.

Fahrenheit : A scale on a thermometer where the freezing point of water is represented by 32 degrees and the boiling point is represented by 212 degrees.

Fahrenheit Temperature Scale : A temperature scale on which the freezing point of water is 32° F and the boiling point is 212° F.

Faint Object Camera (FOC) : An instrument aboard the Hubble Space Telescope that recorded high-resolution images of faint celestial objects in deep space. Built by the European Space Agency, the camera collected ultraviolet and visible light from celestial objects. The camera served as Hubble's "telephoto lens" — recording the most detailed images over a small field of view. The FOC's resolution allowed Hubble to single out individual stars in distant star clusters.

The instrument was replaced in March 2002 during Servicing Mission 3B.

Faint Object Spectrograph (FOS) : An instrument aboard the Hubble Space Telescope that acted like a prism to separate light from the cosmos into its component colors, providing a wavelength "fingerprint" of the object being observed. Such information yields clues about an object's temperature, chemical composition, density, and motion. Spectrographic observations also reveal changes in celestial objects as the universe evolves. The instrument was replaced in February 1997 during the Second Servicing Mission.

Far-Infrared Spectrum : The region of the infrared spectrum that exhibits the longest wavelengths and the lowest frequencies and energies.

Farrum : Pancake-like structure

Fault : A crack or break in the crust of a planet along which slippage or movement can take place. A geological term that refers to a fracture or a break in a hard surface like the Earth's crust. This area is a zone of weakness and may be the site of earthquakes or volcanoes. All planets or moons with a hard crust are candidates for faults or breaks on their surfaces.

Fax : Facsimile transfer (or telegraphy), in which the entire content of a sheet of paper (including diagrams, letterhead, signature and so on) is scanned, coded and sent to a compatible remote terminal connected by a telecommunications link.

FDM : Frequency division multiplexing.

Feedback : The transfer of information from the output of a device or system to the input in such a way as to control the action of the device or system.

Fermions : Particles which obey Fermi-Dirac statistics.

Fibre Optics : The use of ultra-thin flexible strands of very pure glass to carry information at high speed.

Fibril . A linear pattern in the H-ALPHA CHROMOSPHERE of the sun, as seen Through an H-alpha filter, occurring near strong SUNSPOTS and PLAGE or in FILAMENT channels.

Field : One complete scan of a television screen, covering every alternate line; two interlaced fields together make a single frame. The term also refers to a single item of information in a database, such as a name or address; each field may need a large number of bytes to store its information.

Field of View (FOV) : A telescope's viewing area, measured in degrees, arc minutes, or arc seconds. A telescope that can just fit the full moon into its complete viewing area has a field of view of roughly 30 arc minutes.

Filament : A mass of gas suspended over the PHOTOSPHERE by magnetic fields And seen as dark lines threaded over the solar DISK. A filament on the LIMB of the sun seen in emission against the dark sky is Called a PROMINENCE.

A strand of cool gas suspended over the photosphere by magnetic fields, which appears dark as seen against the disk of the Sun; a filament on the limb of the Sun seen in emission against the dark sky is called a prominence.

Filament channel : A broad pattern of FIBRILS in the CHROMOSPHERE, marking Where a FILAMENT may soon form or where a filament recently Disappeared.

File : File Manager

Filename : The name by which a computer system knows a file, perhaps an abbreviation of the one by which the user normally refers to it.

Filter : A type of window that absorbs certain colors of light while allowing others to pass through. Astronomers use filters to observe how celestial objects appear in certain colors of light or to reduce the light of exceptionally bright objects. For example, a pair of sunglasses acts as a type of filter, reducing the amount of incoming light while still allowing some light to pass through to the eyes.

Filter Wheels : Rotating wheels in a telescope instrument that allow specific colors of light from a celestial object to pass through and form an image on the detector. The Wide Field and Planetary Camera 2 aboard the Hubble Space Telescope has 12 filter wheels, each of which holds four filters.

Fine Guidance Sensors (FGS) : Targeting devices aboard the Hubble Space Telescope that lock onto "guide stars" and measure their positions relative to the object being viewed. Adjustments based on these precise readings keep Hubble pointed in the right direction. The sensors also are used to perform celestial measurements.

Fine Motor Skills : Development of the small muscle group, such as fingers, through activity.

Fireball : 1. A bright meteor with an apparent visual magnitude of -4 mag. Or brighter. 2. A meteor brighter than magnitude -3

Firmware : Intermediate between software and hardware, firmware instructions are fitted in to a computer semi-permanently, usually in the form of ROM chips.

Fission : A nuclear process that releases energy when heavyweight atomic nuclei break down into lighter nuclei. Fission is the basis of the atomic bomb.

The release of nuclear energy by the breaking apart of large, heavy elements (e.g. Uranium) into two or more smaller atoms. Nuclear fission is the basis for so-called A bombs, and for nuclear power reactors.

Fissure : A narrow opening or crack of considerable length and depth.

Fixed Head Star Trackers (FHST) **:** Small telescopes with wide fields of view that are aboard the Hubble Space Telescope and used in conjunction with the Fine Guidance Sensors. The star trackers locate the bright stars that are used to orient the telescope for scientific observations.

Flare : A sudden eruption of energy on the solar DISK lasting minutes to Hours, from which radiation and particles are emitted.

Flat Universe : A geometric model of the universe in which the laws of geometry are like those that would apply on a flat surface such as a table top.

Flexion : Bending of a joint.

Flexus : A cuspate linear feature. Cuspate (pointed) linear feature.

Floppy Disc (Floppy) : See disc.

Flowchart : Method of showing the logic of a computer programme or the sequence of operations in a system using boxes joined with arrowed lines.

Fluctus : Flow terrain.

Flux : A flux is the rate at which something is transferred through a surface, like 10 flies per minute through the busted screen door. In astronomy we use flux to express the amount of energy radiated per second across an area like a square centimeter.

The flow of fluid, particles, or energy through a given area within a certain time. In astronomy, this term is often used to describe the rate at which light flows. For example, the amount of light (photons) striking a single square centimeter of a detector in one second is its flux.

FM : Frequency modulation.

Fmin : The lowest radiowave frequency that can be reflected from the ionosphere.

Focal Length : The distance between the center of a reflecting surface (or refracting medium) and the focal point.

Focal Point : The point where parallel beams are brought together (into *focus*) by a convex lens or a concave mirror (or other reflecting surface.)

Foes : The maximum ordinary mode radiowave frequency capable of reflec-tion from the sporadice region of the IONOSPHERE.

Fof 2 : The maximum ordinary mode radiowave frequency capable of reflec-tion from the F2 region of the ionosphere.

Footprint : The area of the earth's surface with which a satellite can communicate, or the area of a surface that an item of equipment occupies.

Forbush decrease : An abrupt decrease, of at least 10%, of the backgroundGalactic COSMIC RAY intensity as observed by neutron monitors.

Format : The format of a piece of text means its headings, spacing, layout and margins. The format of data means its arrangement in a file, on a disc or on a screen. The format of a video tape or video disc includes its physical size and colour standard. As a verb, to format a disc is to prepare it to receive information in the form suited to the system in use; this process deletes any information which was on the disc before.

Fossa : A long, narrow, shallow depression.

Fourth Generation : The imminent style of computer use, with VLSI electronics, parallel processing and human/machine communication by speech, and with software giving freer use of natural language than at present.

Frame : A complete video picture, made up of two fields, in videotex, a single screenful of information; in microform, a single image.

Frame Grabber : A device that captures a frame from a television signal and turns it into digital form so that a computer can store, display and manipulate it.

Franklin, Benjamin 1706-1790 **:** American public official, writer, and scientist. Played a major part in the American Revolution and helped draft the Constitution. His numerous scientific and practical innovations include the lightning rod, bifocal spectacles, and a stove. French astronomer and physicist and Director of the Paris Observatory, who discovered the phenomenon of the production of magnetism by rotation

Freeze Frame : A single frame from a moving sequence held motionless on screen, though not designed to be viewed in isolation (contrast still frame).

Frequency : Describes the number of wave crests passing by a fixed point in a given time period (usually one second). Frequency is measured in Hertz (Hz).

This is a property of a wave, and it is the number of wave crests that pass a given point per second. Frequency is is measured in units of inverse time (e.g., "cycles per second"). A cycle per second is the unit of frequency and it is known as a "Hertz." Since light moves at the constant speed of light, the frequency of a light wave is related to the wavelength: the frequency is given by the number of wavelengths that go by per second at the speed of light, hence frequency is wavelength (distance) divided by speed (c). The higher the frequency of light the greater its energy.

Frequency Division Multiplexing (FDM) : A method of sending several signals clown a single communications channel by letting each source use a different frequency.

Frequency Modulation (FM) : A method of encoding information on a carrier wave by varying its frequency.

Front End : The interface between a hardware and/or software system and its user.

Function Keys : Special keys on a keypad or keyboard that do certain operations at a touch. Sometimes their actions can be defined and redefined by the user, so that the same key which justifies text while word processing might also recalculate a spreadsheet, for instance.

Fusion : A nuclear process that releases energy when light atomic nuclei combine to form heavier nuclei. Fusion is the energy source for stars like our Sun.

A nuclear reaction in which an element with small atoms fuses to form an element with larger atoms, releasing large amounts of energy.

The release of nuclear energy by the fusing or joining together of light elements to form a heavier element. The Sun obtains its central power from the fusing of four hydrogen atoms into one helium atom. Nuclear fusion is a main source of energy in H-bombs. Nuclear fusion is being studied as a possible controlled power source, but this has not yet proven to be feasible.

❑❑❑

G

Gaia Hypothesis : Named for the Greek Earth goddess Gaea, this hypothesis holds that the Earth should be regarded as a living organism. British biologist James Lovelock first advanced this idea in 1969.

Galactic Cannibalism : The (gravitational) swallowing of one galaxy by another. Our own galaxy, the Milky Way, will eventually eat several dwarf galaxies and will probably be eaten by the Andromeda galaxy.

Galactic Center : The central hub or nucleus of a galaxy. The Milky Way's galactic center is about 28,000 light-years from Earth.

Galactic Disk : A flattened disk of gas and young stars in a galaxy. Some galactic disks have material concentrated in spiral arms (as in a spiral galaxy) or bars (as in barred spirals).

Galactic Halo : Spherical regions around spiral galaxies that contain dim stars and globular clusters. The radius of the halo surrounding the Milky Way extends some 50,000 light-years from the galactic center.

Galactic Nucleus : The central concentration of matter (stars, gas, dust, and perhaps a black hole) in a galaxy, typically spanning no more than a few light-years in diameter.

Galactic Plane : The imaginary projection of the Milky Way's disk on the sky. Most of the galaxy's stars and interstellar matter reside in this disk. Objects in the galaxy are often referred to as being above, below, or in the galactic plane

Galaxy : A cluster of stars, dust, and gas held together by gravity.

Collection of stars, gas, and dust bound together by gravity. The smallest galaxies may contain only a few hundred thousand stars, while the largest galaxies have thousands of billions of stars. The Milky Way galaxy contains our solar system.

A large grouping of stars, galaxies may have 10 billion stars in them. And there may be as many as ten billion galaxies in the Universe. Our own galaxy is named the Milky Way, and is a spiral galaxy. Although there are many close dwarf galaxies, the nearest full sized galaxy is named the Andromeda galaxy.

Galaxy Cluster : A collection of dozens to thousands of galaxies bound together by gravity.

Galaxy Evolution : The study of the birth of galaxies and how they change and develop over time.

Galaxy Supercluster : A vast collection of galaxy clusters that may contain tens of thousands of galaxies spanning over a hundred million light-years of space. Galaxy superclusters are the largest structures in the universe.

Galilean Moons : Jupiter's four largest moons: Io, Europa, Ganymede and Callisto; discovered independently by Galileo and Marius. (Galileo proposed that they be named the **Medicean stars**, in honor of his patron Cosimo II de Medici; the present names are due to Marius)

Galileo Galilei 1564-1642 **:** Italian astronomer and physicist. The first to use a telescope to study the stars. Discoverer of the first moons of an extraterrestrial body (see above). Galileo was an outspoken supporter of Copernicus's heliocentric theory. In reaction to Galileo, the Church declared it heresy to teach that the Earth moved and silenced him. The Church clung to this position for 350 years; Galileo was not formally exonerated until 1992.

Galle, Johann Gottfried 1812-1910 : German astronomer who, with Heinrich Louis d'Arrest, made the first observation of Neptune based on calculations by Le Verrier. Though Galle was the first to observe Neptune, its discovery is usually credited to Adams (who made an earlier calculation) and Le Verrier.

Gamma : A unit of magnetic field intensity equal to 1 **x 10.0E-**05 GAUSS, Also equal to 1 NANOTESLA.

Gamma rays : High energy radiation (energies in excess of 100 kev) observedDuring large, extremely energetic solar FLARES. Light with the shortest wavelengths and the highest energies and frequencies in the electromagnetic spectrum; also called gamma radiation. Penetrating short wave electromagnetic radiation of very high frequency.

Gamma-Ray Burst (GRB) **:** A brief, intense, and powerful burst of gamma rays, the highest-energy, shortest-wavelength radiation in the electromagnetic spectrum. These bursts emanate from distant sources outside our galaxy and last only a few seconds. They are the brightest and most energetic explosions known.

An outburst (lasts for a few minutes) of gamma-ray and X-ray which contains energy equal to or greater than a *supernova*.

Ganulation : A pattern of small cells seen on the surface of the Sun caused by the convective motions of the hot solar gas.

Ganymede : One of Jupiter's largest moons. Ganymede, the largest satellite in our solar system, is about 5300 kilometers (3300 miles) wide and larger than the planet Mercury.

Gas Giant Planet : A type of planet characterized by being composed almost entirely of gas. Since gas weighs much less than rock, and since gravity is the reason planets form, gas giant planets are large. Jupiter, Saturn, Uranus, and Neptune are gas giant planets. Gas giant planets are also called Jovian planets.

Gas planet : A planet that has an outer layer of hot gases

Gaseous Nebula : A glowing cloud of gas in interstellar space. The cloud of gas may be either an emission nebula, which absorbs ultraviolet light from nearby stars and re-radiates visible light, or a reflection nebula, which reflects light off of its dust particles.

Gateway : A link that allows certain network or viewdata users access to external computers and their databases.

Gauss. The unit of magnetic induction in the cgs (centimeter-gram- Second) system.

Gegenschein : A round or elongated spot of light in the sky at a point 180 degrees from the Sun. Also called counterglow.

Gene Therapy : An experimental technique that, in hemophilia, involves taking normal genes (the ones that tell the body to make clotting factor) and placing them into the body of a person with hemophilia, in hopes that his body will begin to make clotting factor on its own.

Generation : It is useful to describe the history of the modern computer in four stages or generations. The processors of the first

(1940s and 1950s) were based on valves; those of the second (1960s and early 1970s) used transistors, those of the third (current) have chips; while people expect the hardware of the fourth generation (1990s) to involve a number of processor chips working in parallel.

Geocentric : An adjective meaning "centered on the Earth." Most early civilizations had a geocentric view of the universe.

Earth-centered.

Refers to a reference system centered at the Earth's center. A major difference between geocentric and topocentric ephemerides is that no local horizon exists (and therefore derived quantities such as azimuth and elevation are not defined) for a geocentric ephemeris.

Geodetic coordinates, latitude and longitude, specify a location on the Earth's oblate (non-spherical) surface. Latitude, unless otherwise specified, is generally the geodetic latitude. Geodetic latitude is defined as the angle between the equatorial plane and a line normal to the surface at that location. Geodetic longitude is the angular distance between the location's meridian and the Greenwich meridian.

Geomagnetic elements. The components of the geomagnetic field at the sur- Face of the earth. In SESC use, the northward and eastward Components are often called the H and D components, where the D component is expressed in gammas and is derived from D (the Declination angle) using the small angle approximation.

Geomagnetic field. The magnetic field observed in and around the earth. The intensity of the magnetic field at the earth's surface is Approximately 0.32 gauss at the equator and 0.62 gauss at the North pole.

Geomagnetic storm. A worldwide disturbance of the earth's magnetic field, Distinct from regular diurnal variations. Minor Geomagnetic Storm: A storm for which the Ap index was Greater than 29 and less than 50. Major Geomagnetic Storm: A storm for which the Ap index was Greater than 49 and less than 100.

Geophysical events : Flares (Importance two or larger) with Centimetric Outbursts (maximum of the flux higher than the Quiet Sun flux, Duration longer 10 minutes) and/or strong SID. Sometimes these Flares are followed by Geomagnetic Storms or small PCA. (Class M

Geostationary : If a satellite circles the earth at a height of around 36,000 km (22,000 miles) it takes 24 hours to complete its orbit. It therefore appears to hover over the same place on the earth's surface and is then geostationary.

Geosynchronous : An orbit in which a satellite's rate of revolution matches the Earth's rate of rotation. This allows the satellite to stay over the same site on the Earth's surface at all times.

Term applied to any equatorial satellite with an orbital Velocity equal to the rotational velocity of the earth. The net Effect is that the satellite is virtually motionless with respect To an observer on the ground.

Geosynchronous orbit : A direct, circular, low inclination orbit in which the satellite's orbital velocity is matched to the rotational velocity of the planet; a spacecraft appears to hang motionless above one position of the planet's surface.

Also known as geostationary. An orbit in which an object circles the Earth once every 24 hours, moving at the same speed and direction as the planet's rotation. The object remains nearly stationary above a particular point, as observed from Earth. The International Ultraviolet Explorer (IUE) and some weather satellites are examples of satellites in geosynchronous orbit. German astronomer, known for the bogus "Bode's Law" which attempts to explain the sizes of the planetary orbits.

Giant molecular cloud (GMC) : Huge region of cool clouds of dust grains, and gas (usually in molecular forms). It appears where most of the stars are formed in galaxies.

Giant Molecular Cloud : A region of dense interstellar medium that is sufficiently cold that molecules can form. They are very cold (10-20K) with relatively high densities (trillion particles per cubic meter), and huge. Even though the temperatures are very cold the molecules in these molecular clouds emit radio radiation which can be detected on Earth. These regions are believed to be where new stars can form.

Giant Star : A dying star that has used up the hydrogen fuel in its core and has begun to expand. Giant stars are generally larger than our Sun.

Gigabyte (GB) : Around a thousand million bytes (actually 1, 073, 741, 824 bytes or 1 x 109 bytes).

Gigo : Short for garbage in, garbage out – a long-standing cliche about using computers.

GIPS : Giga-instructions per second: a measure of the speed of a computer processor in units of a thousand million instructions a second.

Global Village : Jargon phrase to describe a possible future in which everyone has access to cheap powerful IT systems linked to all others, so allowing close world-wide contacts and information transfers.

Globular Cluster : A collection of hundreds of thousands of old stars held together by gravity. Globular clusters are usually spherically shaped and are often found in the halos of galaxies. Each star belonging to a cluster revolves around the cluster's common center of mass.

A dense, rich, spherical cluster of stars, held together by their own mutual gravity, and containing up to hundreds of thousands of stars within a diameter of order 100 pc. Globular clusters are generally found in the halo of the Galaxy, and contain old Population II type stars.

Tightly bound, roughly spherical collection of hundreds of thousands, and sometimes millions, of stars spanning about 100 light years.

GMT : Greenwich Mean Time. (See COORDINATED UNIVERSAL TIME.)

Goddard High Resolution Spectrograph (GHRS) **:** A science instrument aboard the Hubble Space Telescope that made finely detailed spectroscopic observations of ultraviolet sources. The GHRS was removed from Hubble in February 1997 and replaced with the Space Telescope Imaging Spectrograph.

Goddard Space Flight Center (GSFC) **:** NASA's flight control center in Greenbelt, Maryland, which receives data from orbiting observatories such as the Hubble Space Telescope (HST). HST digital data are then relayed to the Space Telescope Science Institute in Baltimore, Maryland, where they are interpreted into pictures. Goddard also conducts scientific investigations, develops and operates space systems, and works toward the advancement of space science technologies.

Graben : An elongated, relatively depressed crustal unit or block that is bounded by faults on its sides.

Gradual commencement : The commencement of a geomagnetic storm that has No well-defined onset.

Grand Unified Theory (GUT) **:** A theory stating that that strong and weak nuclear forces and electromagnetic forces are varying aspects of the same fundamental force.

Granulation : A pattern of small cells seen on the surface of the Sun caused by the convective motions of the hot solar gas.

Cellular structure of the PHOTOSPHERE visible at high spatial Resolution.

Graphics : Pictures that a processor can draw on screen or print on to paper. The higher the resolution of the output device the better the picture. Business graphics software allows the user very simply to build up high quality graphs and charts from sets of data.

Gravitational Clustering : The process by which a large-scale structure grows as its gravity attracts smaller building blocks. Astronomers believe that all the large-scale structures (such as galaxies, galaxy clusters, and galaxy superclusters) that we see in the universe today formed through gravitational clustering.

Gravitational Constant (G) **:** A value used in the calculation of the gravitational force between objects. In the equation describing the force of gravity, "G" represents the gravitational constant and is equal to 6.672 10^{-11} Nm^2/kg^2.

Gravitational field : The volume over which an object exerts a gravitational pull.

Gravitational force : See Gravity

Gravitational Instability : A condition that occurs when an object's inward-pulling gravitational forces exceed the outward-pushing pressure forces, thus causing the object to collapse on itself. For example, when the pressure forces within an interstellar gas cloud cannot resist the gravitational forces that act to compress the cloud, then the cloud collapses upon itself to form a star

Gravitational Lens : A massive object that magnifies or distorts the light of objects lying behind it. For example, the powerful gravitational field of a massive cluster of galaxies can bend the light rays from more distant galaxies, just as a camera lens bends light to form a picture.

A massive object which causes light to bend and focus. This occurs because light falls in a gravitational field.

Gravitational pull : See Gravity

Gravitational Radiation : The theory of general relativity predicts that if one changes the distributions of masses (which generate gravitational fields) in certain ways one can get propagating waves of gravity in a manner analogous to the propagating waves of electric and magnetic fields (i.e., light) in the theory of electromagnetism. Gravitational radiation carries energy and travels at the speed of light.

Gravitational Redshift : The reddening of light from a very massive object caused by photons escaping and traveling away from the object's strong gravitational field. An example of gravitational redshift is light escaping from the surface of a neutron star.

Gravity *(Gravitational Force)* **:** The attractive force between all masses in the universe. All objects that have mass possess a gravitational force that attracts all other masses. The more massive the object, the stronger the gravitational force. The closer objects are to each other, the stronger the gravitational attraction.

A mutual physical force attracting two bodies.

The force of attraction between two objects which is influenced by the mass of the two objects and the distance between the two objects.

Gravity Assist : An effect through which an orbiting object, such as a spacecraft or a comet, gains or loses speed by virtue of the gravitational might of a planet or other celestial object that it passes. For example, the Cassini spacecraft in its journey to Saturn used a gravity assist from Earth to increase its velocity by about 36,000 kilometers per hour (22,300 miles per hour).

Gravity, Surface : A spherical object of Mass M and radius R produces a downward gravitational acceleration at its surface (the surface gravity) equal to GM/R^2. Increasing the mass or decreasing the radius will cause the surface gravity to go up. The surface gravity of the Earth (called one "g") is equal to 9.8 meters per second squared.

GRB990123 : One of the most energetic gamma-ray bursts (grbs) ever detected, occurring at 4:47 a.m. EST, January 23, 1999.

The "burst" equaled the power of nearly 10 million billion suns. It became the first GRB to be viewed simultaneously in both gamma-ray and optical wavelengths.

Great Red Spot : A circulating storm located in Jupiter's upper atmosphere. The storm, which rotates around the planet in six days, is the width of two to three Earths. Galileo first observed the spot in the 17th century.

Green Line : The green line is one of the strongest (and first-recognized) Visible coronal lines. It identifies moderate temperature regions of the CORONA.

Greenhouse effect : An increase in temperature caused when the atmosphere absorbs incoming solar radiation but blocks outgoing thermal radiation; carbon dioxide is the major factor.

Increase in temperature caused when incoming solar radiation is passed but outgoing thermal radiation is blocked by the atmosphere (carbon dioxide and water vapor are the major factors). Very important on Venus and Earth but very weak on Mars. Increase in temperature caused when incoming solar radiation is passed but outgoing thermal radiation is blocked by the atmosphere (carbon dioxide and water vapor are the major factors). Very important on Venus and Earth but very weak on Mars.

Gross Motor Skills : Development of the large muscle group, such as legs, arms, and stomach, through activity.

Ground State : The minimum energy state of an atom that is achieved when all of its electrons have the lowest possible energy and therefore are as close to the nucleus as possible.

Ground-Level Event (Gle) : A sharp increase in ground-level cosmic ray count To at least 10% above background, associated with solar protons of Energies greater than 500 mev. Gles are relatively rare, occur- Ring only a few times each solar cycle.

Group Cohesion : Camaraderie built through activities that allow group members to express and be themselves and interact; a unit formed by playing and working together.

Group of Galaxies : A small collection of galaxies bound together by gravity. The number of galaxies in a group can range from a few to dozens. The Milky Way is a member of the Local Group, a collection of more than 30 galaxies.

Guide Star : A star that a telescope's guidance system locks onto to ensure that a celestial object is followed and observed as the telescope moves, owing either to the Earth's rotation or the telescope's orbital trajectory. The Hubble Space Telescope uses two of its three Fine Guidance Sensors to detect and lock onto guide stars. The telescope's science operations center has more than 15 million guide stars in its database — the Guide Star Catalogue.

Guided Imagery : A technique used to help someone focus on various images and pleasant experiences to relieve anxiety, promote relaxation, and provide diversion during painful procedures.

Gyroscope : A heavy wheel or disk mounted so that its axis can turn freely in one or more directions. A spinning gyroscope tends to resist change in the direction of its axis.

A spinning wheel mounted on a non-stationary frame that stabilizes and points a space-based observatory. This spinning wheel resists applied external forces and tends to retain its original orientation in space. For example, balancing on a moving bicycle is easier than balancing on a stationary one because of this tendency. Gyroscopes are used in navigational instruments for aircraft, satellites, and ships. The Hubble Space Telescope has six gyroscopes on board for navigation and sighting purposes.

❑❑❑

H

Habitable Zone : A region around a star where planets with liquid water may be present. A planet on the near edge of the habitable zone would have a surface temperature slightly lower than the boiling point of water. A planet on the distant edge of the habitable zone would have a surface temperature slightly higher than the freezing point of water.

Habitat : The place in which an organism lives and obtains the materials it needs in order to survive.

Hacker : A computer enthusiast, especially one who breaks in to public and private databases. Hacking is sometimes just for fun and sometimes to show how vulnerable the databases are; occasionally it has criminal intentions and effect.

Hadron : A class of particles which participate in the strong interaction (the force that binds atomic nuclei together). Hadrons consist of those particles (baryons, mesons) which are composed of quarks.

Hale, George Ellery 1868-1938 : American astronomer who founded the Yerkes, Mt. Wilson and Palomar observatories.

Half Duplex : A communications line is half duplex when both parties can send and receive information, but not at the same time (contrast duplex and simplex).

Half-Life : The time it takes for half the clotting activity of infused factor to disappear (e.g., a product with a half-life of 12 hours is only half as effective 12 hours after being infused).

Hall, Asaph 1829-1907 : American astronomer who discovered the two moons of Mars, Deimos and Phobos.

Halley, Edmond 1656-1742 : English astronomer who applied Newton's laws of motion to historical comet data and predicted correctly the reappearance of the comet which now bears his name.

Halo, Galactic : An extended region surrounding a galaxy. The halo contains globular clusters and other old stars. The halo apparently has considerable mass but relatively low luminosity, suggesting that a lot of dark matter must be present in the halo.

H-alpha : A narrow wavelength of red light which is emitted and absorbed by the element hydrogen; this wavelength is often used to study the Sun.

This absorption line of neutral hydrogen falls in the red part of The visible spectrum and is convenient for solar observations. The H-alpha line is universally used for patrol observations of Solar flares.

Handshake : The protocols by which two intercommunicating systems or devices check each other's readiness.

Hard Copy : Printed output – jargon for printout.

Hard Disc : A high speed, high density form of external computer memory that can hold much more information than a floppy, but if fixed in the computer (as is common), can't easily be duplicated for back-up.

Hardware : HDTV

H-component of the Geomagnetic Field. See geomagentic clements.

HDF-N : Hubble Deep Field North (HDF-N) is a tiny region of the northern sky near the Big Dipper toward which the Hubble Space Telescope was pointed for ten straight days in 1995. Because this observation was designed to detect very faint light from the most distant galaxies Hubble can observe, the field contains few bright celestial objects. Seemingly devoid of light, this small area provided a "keyhole" view of the universe's past, reaching across space and time to see infant galaxies. By probing these remote regions of space, astronomers are gaining more information on galaxy development.

HDF-S : Hubble Deep Field South (HDF-S) is a tiny region of the southern sky near the Southern Cross toward which the Hubble Space Telescope was pointed for ten straight days in 1998. Because this observation was designed to detect very faint light from the most distant galaxies Hubble can observe, the field contains few bright celestial objects. Seemingly devoid of light, this small area provided a "keyhole" view of the universe's past, reaching across space and time to see infant galaxies. By probing these remote regions of space, astronomers are gaining more information on galaxy development.

Head : The part of a magnetic disc or tape drive or of an optical disc or tape player that allows transfer of data between the storage medium and the system.

Heliocentric : Refers to a reference system centered at the sun. For example, the heliocentric distance to an object is the distance between the object and the sun's center.

An adjective meaning "centered on the Sun."

Having the Sun as a center, such as a heliocentric solar system.

Referring to the sun. A heliocentric orbit is one based on the sun as one of the two foci of the (elliptical) orbit (or as the center of a circular orbit); a heliocentric magnitude is the brightness of an object as would be seen from a heliocentric distance of 1 AU (which means a distance of 1 AU from the sun).

Heliopause : The point at which the solar wind meets the interstellar medium or solar wind from other stars.

Heliosphere : The space within the broundary of the heliopause containing the Sun and solar system.

Helium Flash : In certain low-mass stars when they become red giants their cores are supported by electron-degeneracy pressure. When helium burning begins by the triple-alpha reaction the temperature in the core rises, but the pressure doesn't increase because electron degeneracy pressure is relatively insensitive to pressure. The nuclear reaction rate increases with temperature and a sort of mini explosion occurs. This runaway nuclear reaction finally causes the core to expand a bit, lowering the temperature, leading to a core supported by ordinary pressure, and kept hot by slower, more stable triple-alpha reactions.

Helium Shell Flash : Helium burning in the shell of an triple alpha reaction. The temperature in the shell increases, the burning begins and runs away before the shell can readjust. The shell expands, cutting off the burning entirely. It can never settle down to steady burning. These shell flashes buffet the outer layers of the star and eventually blow those layers away from the star to create a planetary nebula.

Hemisphere : A half of the celestial sphere that is divided into two halves by either the horizon, the celestial equator, or the ecliptic.

Herschel, Sir William 1738-1822 : British astronomer who discovered Uranus and cataloged more than 800 double stars and 2,500 nebulae.

Hertz (Hz) : The unit of frequency, one cycle per second. Radio frequencies are often quoted in kilohertz (thousands of hertz), while processors usually have clock frequencies measured in megahertz (millions of hertz).

Hertzsprung-Russell Diagram : A plot showing the relationship between the brightness (luminosity) and the surface temperatures of many stars. Often the spectral class, which is based on the temperature of the star, is used as a label.

Heuristics : The fuzzy rules of thumb that guide certain artificially intelligent systems.

Hierarchy : An arrangement in which there are several levels, with higher levels more general than lower ones. Hierarchical databases represent the relationships between different levels in their structure.

High Definition TV (HDTV) : A planned international standard for the video systems of the 1990s that offers much higher definition than the current (e.g. 625 line) ones.

High energy event : Flares (class two or more) with outstanding Centimetric Bursts and SID. High Energy Protons are reported at the Earth in Case of most of these events occurring on the western part of solar Disk. (Class X flares)

High frequency (hf) : That portion of the radio frequency spectrum between Between 3 and 30 mhz.

High latitudes : With specific reference to zones of geomagnetic activity, "high latitudes" refers to 50° to 80° geomagnetic.

High Level (Programming) Language : A language like Basic or Cobol, in which instructions are written in words resembling English for subsequent translation into machine code.

High Resolution Graphics : Computer-generated pictures with a lot of detail, which can, for instance, show smooth curves – at least 500 by 500 pixels.

High Speed Photometer (HSP) : An original science instrument aboard the Hubble Space Telescope that made very rapid photometric observations of celestial objects in near-ultraviolet to visible light. The instrument was removed in December 1993 during the First Servicing Mission.

High-pressure mineral phase : In this phase, mineral forms that are stable only at the extremely high pressures typical of Earth's deep interior but not its surface. Such pressures are generated instantaneously during meteorite impact. Stishovite is the high-pressure polymorph of quartz, a common crustal mineral.

High-speed stream : A feature of the solar wind having velocities that are About double average solar wind values.

HII Region : "HII" (pronounced H two) is ionized hydrogen. (The roman numeral refers to the ionization state. I means neutral, II means one electron ionized, III means two electrons ionized, etc. Of course Hydrogen only has one electron, so HII is as high as it gets.) An HII region then is a region of ionized hydrogen in space. When electrons recombine with the hydrogen nuclei, the emit photons, hence an HII region corresponds to an emission nebula.

Home Infusion : Infusion done by a patient or his parents at home, after being trained by a treatment center professional. The main advantage of home infusion is that bleeds can be stopped quickly, resulting in less pain and joint damage.

Homologous flares : Solar flares that occur repetitively in the same active region, with essentially the same position and with a common Pattern of development.

Horizon : The plane tangent to the Earth's surface at an observer's position. See celestial sphere for a helpful diagram.

Horizontal Branch : Stars that are burning Helium in their core lie along a nearly horizontal line in the HR diagram referred to as the Horizontal Branch. It is like the main sequence (which is the line of stars that are burning hydrogen in their cores).

Host : The central storage computer in an electronic mail or viewdata network.

Host Galaxy : A galaxy in which a cosmic phenomenon, such as a supernova explosion or a gamma-ray burst, has occurred.

Hot spot : Center of persistent volcanism, thought to be the surface expression of a rising hot plume in Earth's mantle.

H-R Diagram : A graph that uses two stellar properties, such as luminosity versus surface temperature, as its axes. Individual stars are positioned on the graph according to their properties (Absolute Magnitude, and Spectral type correspond to luminosity and temperature). The resulting graph reveals relationships between a stars luminosity and temperature which in turn allows us to determine derived properties such as the age of the star, its evolutionary phase, its radius, etc.

Hubble Constant (H_o) **:** A number that expresses the rate at which the universe expands with time. H_o appears to be between 60 and 75 kilometers per second per megaparsec.

The constant of proportionality (designated *H*) between recession velocity and distance in the Hubble law. It is a constant of proportionality but not a constant in time, because it can change over the history of the universe.

Hubble Expansion : The observed phenomenon that all galaxies in the Universe (outside the local group of galaxies) appear to be moving away from us, implying that the Universe is expanding. The phenomenon was discovered by Edwin Hubble in 1929. Along with cosmic microwave background and big bang nucleosynthesis, Hubble expansion is considered compelling proof of the big bang theory. For more about Hubble expansion, check out this big bang cosmology primer.

Hubble Law : A linear relationship between the distance to a galaxy (R) and the velocity with which that galaxy is receeding from us (v) due to the overall expansion of the universe. The relation is $v = H_o R$ where H_o is the constant of proportionality known as Hubble's constant. The present "best" value of the Hubble constant is about 70 kilometers per second per Megaparsec.

Hubble Space Telescope (HST) **:** An orbiting telescope that collects light from celestial objects in visible, near-ultraviolet, and near-infrared wavelengths. The telescope was launched April 24, 1990 aboard the NASA Space Shuttle Discovery. The 12.5-ton (11,110-kg), tube-shaped telescope is 13.1 m (43 ft) long and 4.3 m (14 ft) wide. It orbits the Earth every 96 minutes and is mainly powered by the sunlight collected by its two solar arrays. The telescope's primary mirror is 2.4 m (8 ft) wide. The telescope is operated jointly by the National Aeronautics and Space Administration (NASA) and the European Space Agency (ESA). HST is one of the many NASA Origins Missions, which include current satellites such as the Far Ultraviolet Space Explorer (FUSE) and future space observatories such as the Next Generation Space Telescope (NGST).

Hubble Time : The inverse of the Hubble constant. The Hubble time, also called the Hubble age or the Hubble period, provides an estimate for the age of the universe by presuming that the universe has always expanded at the same rate as it is expanding today.

Hubble, Edwin Powell 1889-1953 : American astronomer whose observations proved that galaxies are "island universes", not nebulae inside our own galaxy. His greatest discovery was the linear relationship between a galaxy's distance and the speed with which it is moving. The Hubble Space Telescope is named in his honor.

Hubble's Law : Mathematically expresses the idea that the recessional velocities of faraway galaxies are directly proportional to their distance from us. Hubble's Law describes the relationship of velocity and distance by the equation $V=H_0 * d$, where V is the object's recessional velocity, d is the distance to the object, and H_0 is the Hubble constant. Essentially, the more distant two galaxies are from each other, the faster they are traveling away from each other. American astronomer Edwin Hubble discovered this relationship in 1929 when he observed that galaxies and clusters of galaxies were generally moving away from each other.

Hummocky : Uneven, lumpy terrain.

Huygens, Christiaan 1629-1695 : Dutch physicist and astronomer who first described the nature of Saturn's rings (1655) and discovered its moon Titan; also pioneered the use of the pendulum in clocks.

Hybrid : Describes a computer whose architecture includes both analog and digital circuits; a network with a mixture of star, bus and ring sections; a video or compact disc that carries a digital version of analog information or vice versa.

Hyder flare. A filament-associated , often occurring in Spotless regions. The flare presumably results from the impact on the chromosphere of infalling filament material.

Hydrostatic equilibrium : In hydrostatic equilibrium, the pressure outward is balanced by the force of gravity inward. It is an important element in our analysis of the structure of stars. This refers to the balancing of forces in a fluid (fluid=hydro, static=stationary, equilibrium=balance). Stars exhibit hydrostatic equilibrium because while they have enormous self-gravitational forces pulling them together, there is a substantial pressure force pushing up, preventing the star's collapse. If hydrostatic equilibrium is lost the star will expand or contract depending upon which force is larger.

❑❑❑

I

IC : Integrated circuit.

Ice : Planetary scientists use this word to refer to water, methane, and ammonia, which usually occur as solids in the outer solar system.

Icon : A picture or graphic symbol that represents a particular function, for instance, a rubbish-bin icon to let you delete a file.

Igneous : Rock or mineral that solidified from molten or partly molten material.

Iirregular galaxy : The irregular galaxies, as the name implies, have no regular shapes. They are generally high in gas although the amount of dust is quite variable. They have the youngest stellar populations and are actively forming stars.

Image Intensifier : A device capable of intensifying light from a faint source so that it may be more easily detected.

Impact : When one body strikes another with great force. Some examples include a meteor colliding with the Moon or a comet, such as Shoemaker-Levy 9, slamming into Jupiter.

Impact Event : Craters which are the result of a collision between a large body, such as a planet or satellite, and a smaller body such as an asteroid or meteorite. A collision between two solar system bodies that releases exceptionally large amounts of energy. Some examples are the 1908 Siberian Tunguska impact by a comet or an asteroid and the asteroid that struck Earth 65 million years ago, which may have led to the extinction of the dinosaurs and other species of the Cretaceous-Tertiary era.

Impact melt : Rocks melted during impact, including small particles dispersed in various impact deposits and ejecta, and larger pools and sheets of melt that coalesce in low areas within the crater.

Impact melts are extremely uniform in their composition but highly variable in texture. They are composed predominantly of the target rocks, but can contain a small but measurable amount of the impactor.

Inclination : The angle between the vectors normal to the body's orbit plane and the specified reference plane. Typical reference planes are the ecliptic plane and the equatorial plane (referred to a specific epoch).

The inclination of a planet's orbit is the angle between the plane of its orbit and the ecliptic; the inclination of a moon's orbit is the angle between the plane of its orbit and the plane of its primary's equator.

Infection Prevention : Actions taken to reduce the likelihood of infection, such as disposing of used needles properly and washing hands thoroughly with soap and water.

Inferior planets : The planets Mercury and Venus are called inferior planets because their orbits are closer to the Sun than is Earth's orbit. (The other planets are called "superior" planets.)

Inflation : The theory that the universe expanded very rapidly shortly after the Big Bang.

A theory proposed by Alan Guth in 1980 which suggests that the size of the early Universe greatly increased in a very short period of time. Although the theory is unverifiable, it is widely accepted within the astrophysics community because of its ability to explain certain difficulties.

Information : That which adds to knowledge, data with meaning.

Information Provider (IP) : An individual or organization providing data for a database, usually in the context of viewdata systems, but in general an electronic publisher.

Information Technology (IT) : Includes modern methods of collecting, handling, storing, and passing information, as text, graphics or sound, in this book taken to consist of computing, electronics and telecommunications. The UNESCO definition is: the scientific, technological and engineering disciplines and the management techniques used in information handling and processing; their applications, computers and their interaction with people and machines; and associated social, economic and cultural matters.

Infrared : Radiation that has longer wavelengths and lower frequencies and energies than visible light.

Region of the electromagntic spectrum located just outside visible light, correponding to a light of a slightly longer wavelength than red light.

Infrared Telescope : An instrument that collects the infrared radiation emitted by celestial objects. There are several Earth- and space-based infrared observatories. The Infrared Telescope Facility, an Earth-bound infrared telescope, is the U.S. national infrared observing facility at the summit of Mauna Kea, Hawaii. A planned space-based infrared observatory is the Space Infrared Telescope Facility (SIRTF).

Infrared waves : Electromagnetic radiation with long wavelengths which is found in the invisible part of the spectrum. Human beings experience infrared waves as heat.

Infusion : The injection of medication directly into a vein.

Inhibitors : Antibodies in the blood that react to infused factor and hinder clotting.

Initial Mass Function (IMF) **:** The distribution of masses created by the process of star formation. This function, developed from observation of many stars, tells you how many stars of a given mass there should be in a population of stars. Basically there are few massive stars and many low mass stars.

Initial Phase : Of a geomagnetic storm, that period when there May be an increase of the middle-latitude horizontal Intensity (H).

Inkjet : The mechanism of a compact, fast, quiet printer which sprays tiny drops of ink on to the paper.

Input : Anything put in to a system; also used as a verb meaning to feed in. A keyboard is an example of an input device.

Inquisition : The A Renaissance Catholic court instituted to seek out and prosecute heretics.

Integrated Circuit (IC) : Chip.

Integrated Services Digital Network (ISDN) : A type of digital network that combines voice and data traffic at 64,000 bits a second, so as to allow a wide range of communications options. For instance, subscribers can call up information from a remote computer database using a data channel, and discuss it with a colleague using a high quality voice channel at the same time.

Integrated Software : Programmes designed as a collection so that the output of one can automatically feed into a second.

Intelligence : Describes the ability to do things unpredictably and/or without following clear rules, perhaps with insight and/or inspiration, plus the ability to learn.

Intelligent Device : A stand-alone or peripheral unit with its own (local) processing power.

Intensity : The amount, degree, or quantity of energy passing through a point per unit time. For example, the intensity of light that Earth receives from the Sun is far greater than that from any other star because the Sun is the closest star to us.

Interactive : Interactive communication is two-way so that what one party does depends on the response just received from the other, and vice versa. Interactive computing is the opposite of batch processing. Interactive videotex is viewdata.

Interactive Video (IV) : A new communications medium combining features of computing with features of video presentation. Instead of viewing a programme (a linear sequence of pictures and sound planned in advance by the producers), users choose their own route through the material. They may view still or moving video, hear stereo or dual sound, or see and hear material and sounds generated by computer. Sometimes they may see and hear a combined effect such as computer graphics with video sound, or computer subtitles overlaid on to a video still.

Interactive Videotex : Another name for viewdata.

Interface : The join between two things – a beach is the interface between sea and land. To interface two devices is to do whatever is needed to let them transfer data. Computer interfaces often involve software as well as chips, plugs and cables, and can be costly.

Interference : Loss or alteration of a signal caused by noise (other unwanted signals).

Interference, Wave : A wave is something that moves along and has high points (crests) and low points (troughs). If two (or more) different wave trains pass over one another the crests and troughs can add together to make bigger crests and troughs, and a crest and a trough can add together to produce zero. So if light is a wave phenomenon, then two light sources produce waves that in some places produce large amplitudes and other places produce zero. When to point sources of light are projected onto a screen this wave interference effect produces alternating light and dark spots. This demonstrates the wavelike nature of light.

Interferometer : An instrument that combines the signal from two or more telescopes to produce a sharper image than the telescopes could achieve separately.

Interlace : The process of linking two video fields together to make a complete frame.

Internal Memory : The main store for information inside a system can be of two types: RAM and ROM. Internal memory is faster in use than external memory, but more limited and expensive.

International Ultraviolet Explorer (IUE) : The longest operating (1978—1996) and most productive ultraviolet space observatory launched into a high geosynchronous orbit.

Interplanetary magnetic field (IMF) : The magnetic field carried with the solar wind.

Interplanetary Matter : Dust, gas, and other debris found within the solar system.

Interplanetary Space : The region of space surrounding our Sun. Asteroids, comets, Earth, and the solar wind are examples of things occupying interplanetary space.

Interpreter : Software that translates a programme written in a high level language like Basic, instruction by instruction into machine code, with the result that each line of an interpreted programme has to be retranslated each time it is to be carried out (compare with compiler).

Interstellar absorption lines : Studies of stellar spectra often reveal absorption lines (primarily of sodium and calcium) which clearly arise in the interstellar material (they require low temperatures and they do not show the same radial velocity as the star being studied). They are indicators of the presence of these elements in the interstellar medium and the conditions which cause the absorptions to occur. [See classification of stellar spectra above.]

Interstellar Dust : Small particles of soiid matter, similar to smoke, in the space between stars.

Interstellar Extinction : As light from a star travels through interstellar space it encounters some amount of dust. This dust scatters some of the light, causing the total intensity of the light to diminish. The more dust, the dimmer the star will appear. It is important to take this effect into account when measuring the apparent magnitude of stars. The dark bands running across portions of the milky way in the sky are due to extinction by copious amounts of dust in the plane of our galaxy.

Interstellar Medium (ISM) **:** The sparse gas and dust located between the stars of a galaxy.

The name given to the stuff that floats in space between the stars. It consists of gas (mostly hydrogen) and dust. Even at its densest the interstellar medium is emptier than the best vacuum humanity can create in the laboratory, but because space is so vast, the interstellar medium still adds up to a huge amount of mass.

Interstellar Reddening : As light from a star travels through interstellar space it encounters some amount of dust. This dust scatters some of the light, preferentially the short wavelength (blue) components. The spectrum of the light that remains is increasingly dominated by the long wavelength (red) end of the spectrum, hence the light is "reddened" as it travels through space. It is important to take this effect into account when measuring the color indices of stars.

While dust obscures the light of distant stars, it does so in a manner which is strongly dependent on the wavelength. Thus, the longer wavelengths pass through much more readily than shorter ones. This process leads to a "reddening" of the light, similar to the reddening of sunlight at sunrise and sunset when it is seen through the maximum length of dust in the lower atmosphere. This stellar reddening fortunately allows us to correct the observations to calculate what the colour and magnitude of an object would be in the absence of dust.

Interstellar Space : The dark regions of space located between the stars.

Inventory Software : An advanced type of stock control software that offers some accounts features.

Inverse Square Law : A law that describes any quantity, such as gravitational force, that decreases with the square of the distance between two objects. For example, if the distance between two objects is doubled, then the gravitational force exerted between them is one-fourth as strong. Likewise, if the distance to a star is doubled, then its apparent brightness is only one-fourth as great.

Invisible Radiation : Radiation that the eye cannot detect, such as gamma rays, radio waves, ultraviolet light, and X-rays.

Io : The innermost of Jupiter's four large moons. Due to Jupiter's gravitational might, Io is geologically active; its surface is peppered with volcanoes that send sulfurous eruptions into its thin atmosphere. Io appears to have the most active volcanoes in the solar system.

Io Plasma Torus : A bagel-shaped region of trapped sulfur ions around Jupiter that originates from the surface of Io, one of Jupiter's moons. Gravitational tidal forces between Jupiter, other Galilean moons, and Io cause tidal friction in Io's interior, producing geysers that spew sulfur at tremendous speeds. Some of the sulfur ions leave Io's surface and become trapped around Jupiter.

Ion : An atom or molecular fragment that has a positive electrical charge due to the loss of one or more electrons; the simplest ion is the hydrogen nucleus, a single proton.

Ionization : The process by which ions are produced, typically by collisions with other atoms or electrons, or by absorption of electromagnetic radiation.

Ionization of an electron : See Balmer lines above. Note that unlike bound atoms, free electrons can absorb (or emit) photons at any wavelength.

Ionosphere : A region of charged particles in a planet's upper atmosphere; the part of the earth's atmosphere beginning at an altitude of about 400 kilometers (25 miles) and extending outward 400 kilometers (250 miles) or more.

An upper level of the atmosphere where ions and electrons can be separated.

The region of the earth's upper atmosphere containing a small Percentage of free electrons and ions produced by photoioniza- Tion of the constituents of the atmosphere by solar ultraviolet Radiation at very short wavelengths (l.t.1000 angstroms). The Ionosphere significantly influences radiowave propagation of frequencies less than about 30 mhz.

Ionospheric storm : A disturbance in the F Region of the inosphere, which Occurs in connection with geomagnetic activity.

IP : Information provider.

IPS : Instructions per second: a crude measure of computing power, especially applied to mainframe computers, though normally quoted in KIPS or MIPS (thousands or millions of IPS).

IPSS : International packet switching service: an international network for computer communications that gives higher speeds and reliability than the public telephone network, often at lower cost.

Irregular Galaxy : A galaxy that appears disorganized and disordered, without a distinct spiral or elliptical shape. Irregular galaxies are usually rich in interstellar matter, such as dust and gas. The Large and Small Magellanic Clouds are examples of nearby irregular galaxies.

A galaxy type from the Hubble classification scheme. These galaxies tend to smaller than others, containing 100 million to 10 billion stars, with an irregular overall shape.

A weird shaped galaxy, often rich in interstellar matter, but does not belong to any of the major classes of spiral or elliptical galaxies.

The irregular galaxies, as the name implies, have no regular shapes. They are generally high in gas although the amount of dust is quite variable. They have the youngest stellar populations and are actively forming stars.

Irregular Galaxy Cluster : Clusters of galaxies that are not too centrally condensed, with a somewhat nonspherical overall shape, containing a few galaxies up to hundreds of galaxies. Our local group is an example of an irregular cluster of galaxies. Clusters of galaxies contain all types of galaxies; despite the name, this type of cluster contains more than "irregular galaxies."

ISDN : Integrated services digital network.

Isotope : An atom of a given element having a particular number of neutrons in the nucleus. Isotopes of a given element differ in the numbers of neutrons within the nucleus. Adding or subtracting a neutron from the nucleus changes an atom's mass but does not affect its basic chemical properties.

IT : Information technology.

IV : Interactive video.

❑❑❑

J

Jacket : A type of microform holder which contains short strips of microfilm making the contents simpler to change.

Jets : Narrow, high-energy streams of gas and other particles generally ejected in two opposite directions from some central source. Jets appear to originate in the vicinity of an extremely dense object, such as a black hole, pulsar, or protostar, with a surrounding accretion disk. These jets are thought to be perpendicular to the plane of the accretion disk.

Jets, Radio : Narrow, collimated beams of plasma that are producing radio (synchrotron) emission. These jets emerge from the cores of radio galaxies and can extend outward across regions of space larger than the size of the galaxy itself. These jets are believed to be powered and launched from an accretion disk orbiting a supermassive black hole at the galaxy's core.

Joint Health : The proper functioning and lack of disease of a joint; prompt infusions after joint injuries and regular physical activity promote joint health.

Jovian Atmosphere : The atmosphere surrounding the giant, massive planet Jupiter. The Jovian atmosphere is composed primarily of hydrogen (90 percent) and helium (10 percent). Other minor ingredients include water, hydrogen sulfide, methane, and ammonia.

Jovian Planets : The planets Jupiter, Saturn, Uranus, and Neptune. They are called Jovian planets because of similarities in their composition and location. This group is also known as the "giant planets," the "gas planets" and, when grouped with the planet Pluto, the "outer planets."

Jovian Winds : The hurricane-force, high-velocity motion of gas molecules in Jupiter's atmosphere. The wind speed increases as one travels deeper into Jupiter's atmosphere. The various patterns of atmospheric winds are easily identified in Jupiter's upper cloud layer.

Joystick : A computer input device that consists of a short lever which you can move freely in any direction, often used in place of a keyboard with computer software and interactive video, and also known as a paddle.

Jukebox : A device that contains a bank of discs and can load any one into a drive or player.

Julian date (JD) : The interval of time in days (and fraction of a day) since Greenwich noon on Jan. 1, 4713 BC. The JD is always half a day off from Universal Time, because the current definition of JD was introduced when the astronomical day was defined to start at noon (prior to 1925) instead of midnight. Thus, 1995 Oct. 10.0 UT = JD 2450000.5.

Julian year : Exactly 365.25 days, in which a century (100 years) is exactly 36525 days and in which 1900.0 corresponds exactly to 1900 January 0.5 (from the Julian-date system, which is half a day different from civil time or UT). The standard epoch J2000.0, now used for new star-position catalogues and in solar-system-orbital calculations, means 2000 Jan. 1.5 Barycentric Dynamical Time (TDB) = Julian Date 2451545.0 TDB. When this dynamical, artificial "Julian year" is employed, a letter "J" prefixes the year.

Jupiter : The fifth planet from the Sun and the largest planet in our solar system, twice as massive as all the other planets combined. Jupiter is a gaseous planet with a very faint ring system. Four large moons and numerous smaller moons orbit the planet. Jupiter is more than five times the Earth's distance from the Sun. It completes an orbit around the Sun in about 12 Earth years.

With an orbit of 778 million km, and a diameter of 143,000 km, Jupiter is the largest planet in our solar system. It is a gas giant planet. Four of its moons (Io, Europa, Ganymede and Callisto) are visible with binoculars. Check out SEDS' , for more about Jupiter. Or see stardate's Solar System Guide.

Justify : Most typewriters produce text that is unjustified, i.e. has a ragged right-hand edge. Word processing software can rearrange the spaces automatically, justifying the text so that the right margin is straight.

K

K Corona : Of the white-light CORONA (that is, the corona seen by the eye at a Total solar eclipse), that portion which is caused by sunlight Scattered by electrons in the hot outer atmosphere of the sun.

K Index : A 3-hourly quasi-logarithmic local index of geomagnetic activity Relative to an assumed quiet-day curve for the recording site. Range is from 0 to 9. The K index measures the deviation of the Most disturbed horizontal component.

K or KB : Kilobyte, a thousand (strictly 1024) bytes.

KBES : Knowledge-based expert system (see expert system).

Keck Observatory : Two telescopes known as the world's largest optical and infrared telescopes, jointly operated by the California Institute of Technology and the University of California. The telescopes comprise the W.M. Keck Observatory and are located on the summit of Hawaii's dormant Mauna Kea volcano.

Keeler, James E. 1857-1900 **:** American astrophysicist, probable discoverer of the dark narrow gap in the outer part of the A ring of Saturn, and the second director of Lick Observatory. Keeler was (probably accidentally) cheated of his rightful fame when the A ring gap became known as "Encke's Division". Encke had earlier seen a broad, poor contrast feature in the A-ring (now called the "Encke Minimum") which is quite different from the sharp, distinct gap that Keeler recorded on the very first night of observing with the Lick 36-inch refractor. On the other hand, the gap may have been seen even earlier by Francesco De Vico, William Lassell and the Rev. William R. Dawes.

Kelvin : A unit of absolute temperature. A scale for measuring temperature where 0 Kelvin is equal to -273.16 degrees Celsius. Zero

Kelvin is referred to as *absolute zero*, the point at which all motion within molecules comes to a stop.

Kelvin Scale : The temperature scale most commonly used in science, on which absolute zero is the lowest possible value. On this scale, water freezes at 273 K and boils at 373 K.

This is the temperature scale which uses the same size of degree as the Celsius or Centigrade system, but which begins at absolute zero, the coldest temperature possible corresponding to the lowest possible energy state of a system. Temperature in degrees Kelvin gives a measure of the average energy of a system.

Kelvin-Helmholtz contraction : In attempting to determine how the Sun might produce energy at its current rate for the long periods of time suggested by the age of the Earth, Kelvin and Helmholtz in the middle of the 19th century proposed that the Sun could release gravitational potential energy by contracting. This energy could then be released as radiation. Their calculations showed that such a process could provide the solar energy for about 100 million years, not enough for the current solar age of 4.5 billion years. This mechanism is critical, however, in triggering various stages of nuclear fusion generation in stars.

Kepler, Johannes 1571-1630 **:** German astronomer and mathematician. Considered a founder of modern astronomy. Using the positional data carefully amassed by Tycho Brahe, Kepler formulated the famous three laws of planetary motion. They comprise a quantitative formulation of Copernicus's theory that the planets revolve around the Sun.

Kepler's first law: The orbits of planets are ellipses, with the Sun at one focus. Therefore, each planet moves in an elliptical orbit around the Sun.

Kepler's Laws : Three laws, derived by 17th century German astronomer Johannes Kepler, that describe planetary motion.

Kepler's second law: An imaginary line connecting any planet to the Sun sweeps over equaareas in equal intervals of time.

Key : A button switch on a small keyboard called a keypad, a field through which one searches a file or database for specific types of data; or a string used to decode encrypted data.

Key System : A form of local telephone network whose users can each take on some of the roles of a switchboard operator and whose handsets offer a wide range of features.

Keyword : Some databases can be searched by keywords that 'unlock' their contents; the system knows each item by a number of keywords that convey the gist of what it is about. In programming, keywords are instruction words with a special meaning to the computer's programming language.

Kilobyte (K) : Taken to mean 1000 bytes (actually 2^{10} or 1024). Since one byte can store one character, a kilobyte can carry about 150 words of text.

Kilogram (kg) : = 1000 grams = 2.2 pounds, the mass of a liter of water.

Kilometer (km) : A measure of distance in the metric system equal to 1000 meters or about 0.6 of a mile.

KILOMETER : 1000 meters. A kilometer equals 0.6214 miles.

KILOPARSEC : 1000 parsecs. A parsec equals 3.26 light years.

Kinetic Energy : The energy associated with macroscopic motion. In nonrelativistic physics the kinetic energy is equal to one half the mass times the velocity squared, i.e., $1/2\ mv^2$.

KIPS : Knowledge information processing systems: the name given to the next generation of computers to emphasize how different their role will be from traditional computation and data processing.

Kirchhoff's Laws : These are a set of rules for remembering when and why one should observe a continuous spectrum of light, an emission spectrum, and/or an absorption spectrum. Solid bodies or dense gases or liquids give off continuous spectra. Thin cool gas will absorb certain wavelengths of a continuous spectrum of light producing an absorption spectrum. Warm gas emits certain wavelengths producing an emission spectrum. The specific wavelengths emitted or absorbed is uniquely determined by the chemical makeup of the gas. I. A solid, liquid or gas under pressure produces a continuous spectrum (photons at all wavelengths). II. A hot gas (not under pressure) produces an emission spectrum of photons at wavelengths characteristic of the element(s) composing the gas. III. A source of a continuous spectrum, observed through a cooler gas, not under pressure, produces an absorption spectrum (a continuous spectrum except that at wavelengths characteristic of the elements composing the gas the number of photons is reduced by having been absorbed in the gas).

Kitt Peak Observatory : The world's largest collection of telescopes, located high above the Sonora Desert in Arizona. Eight astronomical research institutions share the 22 optical and two radio telescopes at Kitt Peak. The National Optical Astronomy Observatories oversee site operations at the observatory.

Knowledge Engineering : Building up a knowledge-based expert system – the database and the means of access to it.

Kowal, Charles T. 1940- **:** American astronomer; discovered Leda and the comet-like object 2060 Chiron.

Kp Index : A 3-hourly planetary geomagnetic index of activity generated in Gottingen, Germany, based on the K INDEX from 12 or 13 stations Distributed around the world.

Kuiper Belt : A region in our outer solar system where many short-period comets (possessing orbits of less than 200 years) originate. This region begins beyond Neptune's orbit and encompasses an estimated distance of between 30 and 100 astronomical units. There may be as many as 100 million Kuiper belt comets.

Kuiper, Gerard 1905-1973 **:** Dutch-born American astronomer best known for his study of the surface of the Moon; discovered Miranda and Nereid, found an atmosphere on Titan. (Dr.Kuiper was solidly Americanized; his name is pronounced to rhyme with "viper.")

❑❑❑

L

Labes : A landslide.

Labyrinthus : Intersecting valley complex.

Lacus : A lake.

Lagrange points : Lagrange showed that three bodies can lie at the apexes of an equilateral triangle which rotates in its plane. If one of the bodies is sufficiently massive compared with the other two, then the triangular configuration is apparently stable. Bodies at such points are sometimes referred to as Trojans. The

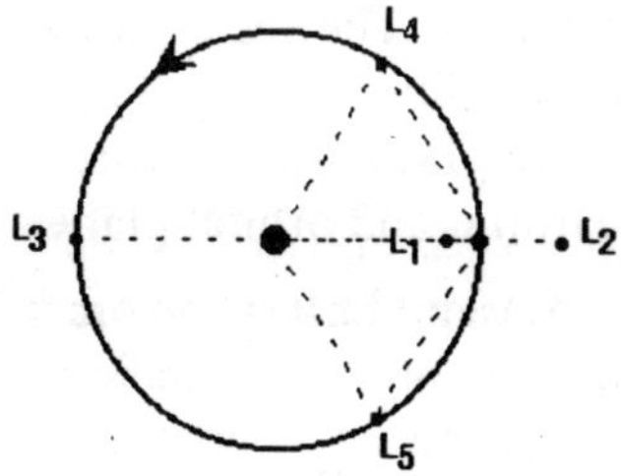

leading apex of the triangle is known as the leading Lagrange point or L4; the trailing apex is the trailing Lagrange point or L5. Collinear with the two large bodies are the L1, L2 and L3 unstable equilibrium points which can sometimes be seful places for spacecraft, eg SOHO.

Lagrangian point : One of the solutions to the three-body problem discovered by the eighteenth century French mathematician Lagrange; the two stable Lagrangian points, L-4 and L-5, lie in the orbit of the primary body, leading and trailing it by a 60-degree arc.

Lagrange, Joseph Louis 1736-1813 : French (originally Italian, Giuseppe Luigi Lagrangia; born in Turin, moved to Paris and became a French citizen) mathematician and astronomer; made a number of contributions to the study of celestial mechanics.

LAN : Local area network.

Land : The smooth raised region between two pits in the surface of a video or compact disc.

Land Line : A telephone cable between two points dedicated to traffic between those points only.

Laplace Plane : The Laplace plane (as used in our satellite orbital elements tables) is defined as the plane in which the satellite's nodal precession is contained (on average). An equivalent definition is the plane normal to the satellite's orbital precession pole. The typical application for the Laplace plane is in describing the orbits of giant-planet satellites which are close enough to the planet to be perturbed primarily by the sun, planet, and the planet's gravitational harmonics. Is such cases, the Laplace plane is constrained to be between the planet's orbital plane and it's equatorial plane. However, in the case of the "outer" Jovian satellites (such as Pasiphae), the perturbations by Saturn and even the Galilean satellites dominate those due to Jupiter's gravitational harmonics. The result of those "external" perturbations (which are not normally considered in typical descriptions of the Laplace plane) is a Laplace plane which is beyond the confines of Jupiter's equatorial and orbital planes.

Laser : Lasers can produce high energy beams of radiation (often light) with important applications in computing and telecommunications. Laser printers are very high speed and high quality page printers. Some video disc systems depend on lasers.

Laser Disc : See optical video disc, though some people use the term for compact disc too. Laservision is a popular type of optical video disc system.

Lassell, William 1799-1880 **:** British astronomer, discovered Neptune's largest satellite, Triton and (with Bond) discovered Saturn's moon Hyperion. A successful brewer before turning to astronomy.

Lava : A general term for molten rock that is extruded onto the surface.

Lava tube : A tunnel formed underneath the surface of a solidfying lava flow.

Layout : The structure and appearance of material on paper or on screen, for instance.

LCD : Liquid crystal display: liquid crystals do not give out light, but can switch from opaque to transparent. This feature can provide quite a legible display in suitable lighting conditions. Such displays need little power, and are used in many lapheld computers as well as in calculators and watches.

Le Verrier, Urbain Jean Joseph 1811-1877 : French mathematician whose prediction of the position of an undiscovered planet (Neptune) that caused perturbations in the orbit of Uranus was the first to be confirmed (by Galle) though Adams had made a similar but unpublished prediction some months earlier.

Leader spot : In a magnetically bipolar or multipolar sunspot group, the Western part precedes and the main spot in that part is called the Leader.

Leading hemisphere : The hemisphere that faces forward, into the direction of motion of a satellite that keeps the same face toward the planet.

LED : Light emitting diode: an element of a display that gives out light when passing an electric current. Such displays are brighter than LCDs, but require more power.

Ledger : A group of accounts with a similar function, such as sales.

Lee : The side of an object that is sheltered from the wind.

Lepton : A member of a class of particles which do not participate in the strong interaction (the force that binds atomic nuclei togeter). The best-known lepton is the electron. Another example is the neutrino.

Levee : An embankment, continuous dike or ridge.

Library : A collection of discs or tapes used by a firm, of programmes and sub-programmes used by a programmer, or of standard designs in software used by a designer.

Lidar : An instrument similar to radar that operates at visible wavelengths.

Light : Electromagnetic radiation that is visible to the eye.

Light bridge : Observed in white light, a bright tongue or streaks penetra- Ting or crossing SUNSPOT umbrae. The appearance of a light bridge Is frequently a sign of impending region division or dissolution.

Light Curve : A plot of the amount of light detected from an object (i.e. The apparent magnitude) as a function of time. Light curves provide evidence of eclipsing binaries, variable stars, and track the progress of nova and supernova explosions.

Light Pen (WAND) : A pointing device which can be used to select from choices displayed on a screen, or (sometimes) to draw shapes directly on to the screen; another type is used as a bar code reader.

Light pollution : The emission of stray light or glare from lighting fixtures in manners that counter the purpose of the light (which is to light what is below); also known as the waste of money and energy in the form of electric light, usually meant in the form of outdoor night lighting. Such light trespass causes severe safety problems for motorists, pedestrians, and cyclists at night from lighting that shines onto streets and highways and sidewalks from poorly-designed or poorly-mounted lighting. Such glare also imposes on privacy, by shining brightly into bedroom windows at night and into backyards where adults and children are trying to observe the night sky. While most people have accepted such bad, glare lighting without question and assumed that nothing could be done about it, dedicated groups of volunteers around the world are now showing that effective laws and guidelines can be instated at the local and regional levels of government (and in planning and engineering offices), which mean that proper outdoor night lighting can be a norm so that everybody benefits — auto drivers, sleeping residents, government budgets, and skygazers alike. Laws mandating full-cutoff light fixtures are already in place in states such as Maine and Connecticut and are pending elsewhere.

Light Year (1 yr) : The distance that light travels in one year, equal to 10,000,000,000,000 (9,500,000,000,000 km) km, or 63,000 AU.

The distance light travels in a year, at the rate of 300,000 kilometers per second (671 million miles per hour); 1 light-year is equivalent to 9.46053e12 km, 5,880,000,000,000 miles or 63,240 AU.

= 9.46053e12 km (= 5,880,000,000,000 miles = 63,239 AU); the distance traveled by light in a year.

The distance that a particle of light (photon) will travel in a year — about 10 trillion kilometers (6 trillion miles). It is a useful unit for measuring distances between stars.

LIMB : The edge of the solar disk.

Limb : The outer edge of the apparent disk of a celestial body

Limb flare : A solar flare seen at the edge (LIMB) of the sun.

Limiting magnitude : Generally denotes the faintest star visible during an observation and evaluates the quality of the sky as well as the observing technique. The magnitude of the faintest meteor visible can be different from the stellar limiting magnitude, particularly for photographic and video observations. Visual observations assume about the same limiting magnitudes for stars and meteors.

Line Printer : A high speed computer printer that prints a whole line, as opposed to a single character or a column of dots, at a time.

Linea : An elongate marking.

Lineament : Linear topographic feature that may depict crustal structure.

Linear : Describes material (e.g. programme or text) through which one can pass by only one route, as opposed to branching.

Lines of constant radius : Because of Stefan's law, you can draw lines (roughly parallel to the main sequence) in an HR diagram such that all the stars falling along those lines would have the same radii. Such lines form a parallel set such that the higher up the diagram they fall, the greater the radii. Equal spacings between the lines correspond to equal ratios in the radii.

List Processing : The processing of data arranged in the form of lists; in word processing, sometimes used to describe the insertion of stored information, such as names and addresses, into mail shots.

Listening Skills : The developed ability to understand and retain what people have said; involves being attentive, asking questions for clarification, and not interrupting.

Liter : = 1000 CM^3 = 1.06 US quarts

Lithosphere : The solid part of a planet's surface, composed of the crust and upper mantle. On Earth, it includes the continents and the sea floor.

Load : To copy data from a backing store (e.g. a disc) in to a computer's main memory.

Lobate : Having lobes or resembling a lobe.

Local : Describes short full-time links between those parts of an IT system that are in effect permanently online.

Local Area Network (LAN) : A method for linking computers and peripherals that are nearby, usually on the same site (contrast wide area network (WAN)).

Local Group : A small cluster of more than 30 galaxies, including the Andromeda galaxy, the Magellanic Clouds, and the Milky Way galaxy.

Local Processing : The use by a peripheral, terminal or networked microcomputer of its own processing power rather than that in the centre of the system.

Log On : To register your presence on a system, perhaps also by identifying yourself as an authorized user.

Logger : (Telephone) call logger, or the same kind of device used in other systems.

Longitude of Perihelion : The sum of the longitude of the ascending node and the argument of perihelion.

Longitude of the Ascending Node : The angle between the reference X-direction (typically the vernal equinox) and the point at which the body passes up (north) through the reference plane. This angle is often referred to as capital omega.

Long-Period Comet : A comet having an orbital period greater than 200 years and usually moving in a highly elliptical, eccentric orbit. Comets have orbits that take them great distances from the Sun. Most long-period comets pass through the inner solar system only once. Hale-Bopp is an example of a long-period comet.

Lookback Time : The time required for light to travel from an emitting object to the receiver. Hence when we look at a distant object we are "looking back" in time.

Loop prominence system (LPS) : A system of loop prominences associated withMajor FLARES.

Low frequency (LF) L : That portion of the radio frequency spectrum from 30 to 300 khz.

Low Resolution Graphics : Crude low detail pictures in which individual pixels are clearly visible, with resolution perhaps as low as 40 pixels across by 20 down, suitable for simple bar charts but not for curves.

Lowell, Percival 1855-1916. : American astronomer. He founded the Lowell Observatory in Arizona (1894), where his studies of Mars led him to believe that the linear markings (first noted by Schiaparelli) on the surface were "canals" and therefore that the planet was inhabited by intelligent beings. His successors later discovered Pluto. (26k gif)

LSI : Large scale integration: method of packing a large number (100 to 1000) of electronic components and their connections on to a single chip (see also VLSI and ULSI).

Luminance : The part of a video signal that carries information about the brightness of each point in a television picture (compare with chrominance, that part which handles colour information).

Luminosity : Defined as the total energy radiated by a star at all wavelengths, in a second. It is one of the basic properties for star characterization. A luminosity classification scheme is used to compare the brightness of stars with the same temperature or *spectral class*. Luminosity class V stars are also known as main-sequence stars because most of the stars fall on this category.

The amount of energy radiated into space every second by a celestial object, such as a star. It is closely related to the absolute brightness of a celestial object.

Total amount of energy radiated per second. It has units of energy per second (e.g. Ergs per second). Since many astronomical objects radiate away energy this is an important characteristic. We compare luminosity of an object to the solar luminosity, the total energy given off per second by the sun. One solar luminosity is 4×10^{33} ergs per second. Luminosity has the same units as Power, e.g. Energy per second. The Watt is the familiar unit of power. For comparison, a 400 Watt light bulb is 10^{-24} solar luminosities.

Luminosity Class : Stars are classified by luminous they are. The various luminosity classes correspond to regions on the HR diagram. The luminosity classes are I - Supergiants, II - Bright giant, III - Giant, IV - Subgiant, V - Main Sequence. The luminosity class was originally based on the width of the observed spectral lines within a given spectral type. Width provides a measure of how fast the atoms are moving (doppler shift) and this in turn provides a measure of the strength of the gravitational field of the star, which then determines whether it is a Giant, Supergiant, etc. The main thing is that there are fundamentally different types of stars and the luminosity class helps us to categorize these different types.

Luminosity Function : The relative number of astronomical objects that have a certain luminosity. In the case of stars, the low luminosity stars are the most abundant, and the number of stars declines rapidly with increasing luminosity.

Lunar Eclipse : A darkening of the Moon, as viewed from Earth, caused when our planet passes between the Sun and the Moon.

Lunar month : The average time between successive new or full moons, equal to 29 days 12 hours 44 minutes. Also called synodic month.

Lyman Limit : A specific wavelength (91.2 nm) that corresponds to the energy needed to ionize a hydrogen atom (13.6 ev). Galactic space is opaque at wavelengths shorter than the Lyman limit. Subsequently, light from cosmic objects at wavelengths less than the Lyman limit is exceedingly difficult to detect.

❑❑❑

M

M 3000 : The optimum HIGH FREQUENCY radio wave with a 3000 km range, which Reflects only once from the IONOSPHERE (single hop transmission).

M_1. : Total, integrated magnitude of a comet's head (meaning coma + nuclear condensation). This can be estimated visually, as the comet's "total visual magnitude". The variable m_1 is usually found in ephemerides predicting a comet's future motion, position on the sky, and brightness. See also definition for "Magnitude", below. [*Note* that m_1 is also used by stellar spectrophotometrists to define a "metal index" on the Stroemgren *ubvy* photometric system.]

M_2: The magnitude value measured (or predicted) for a comet's nuclear condensation. Note that the true comet nucleus is rarely, if ever, directly observed from the earth because of the large amount of gas and dust that is ever-present in the inner coma close to the nucleus, serving to hide the true nucleus' surface. So-called "nuclear magnitudes" are therefore fraught with problems as to true meaning, especially because such nuclear magnitudes are extremely dependent upon instrumentation (aperture, focal-ratio, magnification) and wavelength. Nuclear magnitudes are chiefly used for astrometric purposes, in which predictions are made for the brightness of the comet's nuclear condensation so that astrometrists can gauge how faint the condensation is likely to be and thus how long an exposure is needed to get a good, measurable image. (Astrometrists are only concerned about measuring the nuclear condensation, which is considered to be the site of the main mass of any comet.) See also definition for "Magnitude", below.

Machine Code : The 'language' of binary numbers in which a processor works.

Machine Intelligence : Artificial intelligence.

Machine Readable : Describes data held on paper, for instance, in such a form that a suitable input device can transfer a copy to a computer's memory.

MACHO : Massive Compact Halo Object. Any object such as a white dwarf, neutron star, or black hole that could account for some or all of the dark matter in the halos of galaxies.

Machos : machos are objects about the size of Jupiter. Macho is short for massive Compact Halo Object. Machos are the only type of dark matter for which there is direct evidence.

Macula : A dark spot.

Magellanic Clouds : The Magellanic Clouds are two dwarf irregular galaxies. Known as the Large Magellanic Cloud (LMC) and the Small Magellanic Cloud (SMC), the galaxies are in the Local Group. The closer LMC is 168,000 light-years from Earth. Both galaxies can be observed with the naked eye in the southern night sky.

Magflare : A geomagnetic and/or cosmic storm has been associated with this Flare.

Magma : Molten rock within the crust of a planet that is capable of intrusion into adjacent crustal rocks or extrusion onto the surface. Igneous rocks are derived from magma through solidification and related processes or through eruption of the magma at the surface.

Magnetic (Ink) Character Recognition (MCR or MICR) : Automatic recognition by machine of characters printed in special magnetic ink.

Magnetic bay. A relatively smooth excursion of the H (horizontal) component (see geomagnetic elements) of the geomagnetic field away from and Returning to quiet levels.

Magnetic Field : A region of space in which magnetic forces may be detected or may affect the motion of an electrically charged particle. As with gravity, magnetism has a long-range effect and magnetic fields are associated with many astronomical objects.

The area in which an attractive or repelling force exists between two magnets or in association with the element iron. The Earth's magnetic field is thought to be due tc the liquid iron-nickel which is in its core. This magnetic field protects Earth from constant bombardment by high-energy charged particles.

Magnetic Media : Media on which a system can store data in the form of a magnetic record, in particular tape, disc and stripe.

Magnetic Stripe : See stripe.

Magnetic-Field Lines : Imaginary lines used to visualize a magnetic field. Magnetic field lines are related to the strength of the magnetic object's influence and point in the same direction as a compass needle would.

Magnetogram : Solar magnetograms are a graphic representation of solar mag- Netic field strengths and polarity.

Magnetograph : A special telescope which analyzes the color and polarization of sunlight in order to measure the magnetic field of the Sun.

Magnetopause : The boundary layer between the solar wind and the magneto sphere.

The boundary of the magnetosphere, lying inside the bow shock.

Magnetopshere : A region of space above the Earth's (or other planet's) atmosphere where magnetic fields influence the motions of charged particles. The magnetosphere magnetically deflects or traps charged particles from space that would otherwise bombard the planet's surface.

The magnetic cavity surrounding the earth, carved out of the passing solar wind by virtue of the geomagnetic field, which pre-vents, or at least impedes, the direct entry of the solar wind plasma into the cavity.

The region of space in which a planet's magnetic field dominates that of the solar wind.

Magnetotail : The portion of a planetary magnetosphere which is pushed away from the Sun by the solar wind.

Magnitude : A scale used to measure the brightness of a celestial object. The smaller the magnitude (the more negative), the brighter the object appears to us. Each magnitude is approximately 2.5 times brighter than the next higher magnitude. Example: A magnitude +2 star is about 6.25 times brighter than a magnitude +4 star (2.5 × 2.5).

An astronomical unit of brightness. Originally corresponding to the eye's response to starlight, the magnitude system is logarithmic, with 5 magnitudes corresponding to a factor of 100 in brightness. To further confuse things *larger* magnitudes correspond to *fainter* objects.

The degree of brightness of a celestial body designated on a numerical scale, on which the brightest star has magnitude -1.4 and the faintest visible star has magnitude 6, with the scale rule such that a decrease of one unit represents an increase in apparent brightness by a factor of 2.512. Also called apparent magnitude.

The degree of brightness of a celestial body designated on a numerical scale, on which the brightest star has magnitude -1.4 and the faintest visible star has magnitude 6, with the scale rule such that a decrease of one unit represents an increase in apparent brightness by a factor of 2.512; also called *apparent magnitude*.

The units used to describe brightness of astronomical objects. The smaller the numerical value, the brighter the object. The human eye can detect stars to 6th or 7th magnitude on a dark, clear night far from city lights; in suburbs or cities, stars may only be visible to mag 2 or 3 or 4, due to light pollution. The brightest star, Sirius, shines at visual magnitude -1.5. Jupiter can get about as bright as visual magnitude -3 and Venus as bright as -4. The full moon is near magnitude -13, and the sun near mag -26. Comet C/1996 B2 (Hyakutake) reached magnitude about 0 in late March 1996. The magnitude scale is logarithmic, with a difference of one magnitude corresponding to a change of about 2.5 times in brightness; a change of 5 magnitudes is defined as a change of exactly 100 times in brightness. In the case of comets, we speak of a magnitude that is "integrated" over an observed coma diameter of several arc minutes; this is called the comet's "total (visual) magnitude", and is usually denoted by the variable m_1. Thus, a 7th-magnitude comet is much harder to see than a 7th-magnitude star — the latter having all its light in a pinpoint, and the former having the same amount of light spread out over a large area (imagine defocussing a 7th-magnitude star to the size of a diffuse comet). Typically, however, when comets become very bright, their apparent coma sizes shrink so that the majority of visible light is in a small, intense core of the comet's head (and the comet may appear starlike with a tail emanating from the comet's head).

A word processing facility where details from a file of names and addresses are merged into spaces in standard letters.

Mailbox : Space in the memory of a computer reserved for a user's incoming messages.

Main Phase : Of a geomagnetic storm, that period when the hori- Zontal magnetic field at middle latitudes is generally Decreasing.

Main Sequence : The name given for the line in the H-R diagram along which stars lie that are burning hydrogen in their cores. The majority of a star's lifetime is spent as a main sequence star. Main sequence stars are luminosity class V.

Main Sequence Turnoff : When stars age, they run out of hydrogen in their cores. When that happens they begin to change and they move off the main sequence toward the red giant branch. When a cluster of stars forms, all the stars will be on the main sequence. The more massive stars evolve faster and leave the main sequence. The point on the main sequence where stars have just left (defining the end of the main sequence for that cluster) is the main sequence turnoff point.

Mainframe : A large powerful computer with many users, often spread over a distance, sometimes running a variety of languages and software at the same time (see time sharing).

Main-sequence lifetime : Once a contracting proto star begins to convert H into He, it is said to be on the "main sequence". It will remain there for approximately 90% of its active lifetime until it is forced to change its outward appearance and move up into the giant branch as H-burning slows and no longer provides the internal energy needed to withstand the force of gravity in the core of a star.

Major flare : This flare is the basis for the forecast of geomagstorm, cosmic Storm and/or protons in the earth's vicinity.

Maltron : An experimental keyboard with a more efficient layout than the standard (QWERTY) arrangement.

MAN : Metropolitan area network.

Man/Machine Interface (MMI) : The actual point of contact between a hardware system and its human user.

Mantle : The interior region of a terrestrial (rocky) planet or other solid body that is below the crust and above the core.

The middle layer of a planet located between the crust, or surface, and the core.

MAP : Britain's Microprocessor Awareness Project: a government scheme to aid the introduction of IT into business.

Mare : Latin word for "sea." Galileo thought the dark featureless areas on the Moon were bodies of water, even though the Moon is essentially devoid of liquid water. The term is still applied to the basalt-filled impact basins common on the face of the Moon visible from Earth.

Maria : A dark, flat, large region on the surface of the Moon. The term is also applied to the less well-defined areas on Mars. Although maria literally means "seas," watery regions do not exist on the Moon or Mars. Marias on the Moon may be evidence of past volcanic lava flows.

Marius, Simon 1573-1624 : (a.k.a. Mayr) German astronomer who gave Jupiter's "Galilean" moons their names. He and Galileo both claimed to have discovered them in 1610 and likely did so independently. Marius was also the first to observe the Andromeda Nebula with a telescope and one of the first to observe sunspots. (more)

Mars : The fourth planet in the solar system and the last member of the hard, rocky planets (the inner or terrestrial planets) that orbit close to the Sun. The planet has a thin atmosphere, volcanoes, and numerous valleys. Mars has two moons: Deimos and Phobos.

Marshall Space Flight Center (MSFC) **:** NASA center overseeing the research, development, and implementation of three primary areas essential to space flight: reusable space transportation systems, generation and communication of new scientific knowledge, and management of all space lab activities. Located in Huntsville, Alabama, the center aided in the design, development, and construction of the Hubble Space Telescope.

Maser : A small celestial source of electromagnetic radiation in the microwave range. They have been detected in the atmospheres of old variable stars and molecular clouds associated with newly formed or forming stars.

Mass : A measure of the total amount of matter contained within an object.

The measure of how much "stuff" something has, mass determines the inertia of an object (its resistance to being accelerated by a force) and how much gravitational force it exerts on another object. In pre-Einsteinian physics mass was conserved, neither created nor destroyed. Einstein discovered that mass can be converted into energy and vice versa. The conservation of mass is still a good approximation since mass-energy conversions generally involve relatively small amounts of mass. The mass of astronomical objects is often measure in terms of the Sun's mass. The solar mass is 2×10^{33} grams.

The measure of the amount of matter in an object.

Mass defect : In the process of fusing light elements into heavier ones (or fissioning heavy elements like Uranium into lighter ones) a small amount of mass is loss. It is this mass which is known as the mass defect and which appears in Einstein's equation to produce energy.

Mass Luminosity Relation : A main sequence star's luminosity is roughly proportional to its mass to the 3.5 power: $L \sim M^{3.5}$. This relationship was derived from the observations of the masses of various types of main sequence stars, but it has also been demonstrated by the calculation of stellar models of different massed zero age main sequence stars.

Mastery : Coping effectively and having an expertise in dealing with a set of circumstances. Engaging in experiences that enable children to learn to cope effectively and overcome their fears of the medical environment gives them mastery in that situation. Giving a stuffed bear an infusion using actual infusion supplies can help a child gain mastery over the infusion experience.

Math : The projection of the line of motion of the meteor on the celestial sphere, as seen by the observer.

Matter : Anything which has mass and occupies space.

Matter-Antimatter Annihilation : A highly efficient energy-generation process in which equal amounts of matter and antimatter collide and destroy each other, thus producing a burst of energy.

MB : Megabyte.

MCR : Magnetic character recognition.

Mean Anomaly : The product of an orbiting body's mean motion and time past perihelion passage.

Mean Longitude : The sum of the mean anomaly and the longitude of perihelion.

Mean Motion : The angular speed required for a body to make one orbit around an ideal ellipse with a specific semi-major axis. [1]

Medical Play : Spontaneous and guided play experiences and interactions that focus on health care themes and often include medical/ health care equipment; experiences that allow children to freely explore, manipulate, and play with health-related objects in non-threatening, pleasurable ways.

Medium frequency (MF) : That portion of the radio frequency spectrum from 0.3 To 3 mhz.

Medium Resolution Graphics : Pictures of medium quality, adequate for diagrams but unable to show good curves, technically around 300 pixels across by 200 down.

Megabyte (MB) : Usually taken to mean a million bytes (actually 2^{20} or 1,048,576), just enough to hold the text of this book a couple of times.

Megahertz (MHz) : A measure of frequency in millions of cycles per second.

Megaparsec (MPC) : Equals one million parsecs (3.26 million light-years) and is the unit of distance commonly used to measure the distance between galaxies.

Memory : A computer's memory is a device (or a series of devices) capable of storing information temporarily or permanently. Internal memory contains standing instructions and temporary working space. External (backing) memory stores larger volumes of information for less frequent access.

Mensa : A mesa, flat-topped elevation.

Menu Driven : A style of programme in which the user controls the system by choosing options from a menu, as opposed tó typing in commands (contrast command mode).

Mercury : The closest planet to the Sun. The temperature range on Mercury's surface is the most extreme in the solar system, ranging from about 400° C (750° F) during the day to about –200° C (–300° F) at night. Mercury, which looks like Earth's moon, has virtually no atmosphere, no moons, and no water.

With an orbit of only 58 million km, Mercury is the closest planet to the Sun. It is a terrestrial planet, and has a diameter of about 5000 km. Check out SEDS' Nine Planets, for more about Mercury.

Meridian : A great circle passing through the Earth's rotational poles and through the zenith (the point directly overhead) of a location on the Earth.

An imaginary line connecting the north and south celestial poles and passing through the zenith. See celestial sphere for a helpful diagram.

Mesa : A broad, flattop, erosional hill or mountain, commonly bounded by steep slopes.

Message Switching : A form of transfer of electronic messages by a telephone system, storing the message at any point if all the lines to the next stage are in use, until a line is free. Packet switching is similar in this way.

Astronomers refer to all elements other than hydrogen and helium as "metals" (even though these elements aren't all metals as defined by chemists).

Meteor : (also "shooting star" or "falling star") a bright streak of light in the sky caused by the entry into Earth's atmosphere of a meteoroid or a small icy particle. Very large, bright ones are called fireballs and bolides.

A bright streak of light in the sky caused when a meteoroid enters the Earth's atmosphere. The streak of light is produced from heat generated by the meteoroid traveling into the Earth's atmosphere.

In particular, the light phenomenon which results from the entry into the Earth's atmosphere of a solid particle from space.

Meteoroids which burn up in the atmosphere of a space body, such as the Earth, prior to impacting on the surface.

The luminous phenomenon seen when a meteoroid enters the atmosphere, commonly known as a shooting star.

The trail of light seen in the sky when a meteorite burns up in Earth's atmosphere. Also called shooting stars.

Meteor Shower : A number of meteors with approximately parallel trajectories. The meteors belonging to one shower appear to emanate from their radiant.

Meteorite : A natural object of extraterrestrial origin (meteoroid) that survives passage through the atmosphere and hits the ground.

A part of a meteoroid that survives through the Earth's atmosphere.

A rock of extra-terrestrial origin found on Earth.

Fragments of material that fall from space and impact on other larger space bodies.

Interplanetary material which is pulled into Earth's atmosphere by gravity, and burned up by friction with the atmosphere.

The remains of a meteoroid that plunges to the Earth's surface. A meteorite is a stony or metallic mass of matter that did not completely vaporize when it entered the Earth's atmosphere.

Meteoroid : A small, solid object moving through space. A meteoroid produces a meteor when it enters the Earth's atmosphere.

A solid object moving in interplanetary space, of a size considerably smaller than a asteroid and considerably larger than an atom or molecule.

Ments of material which vaporize when they have a close encounter with a space body which has an atmosphere.

Meteoroid Stream : Stream of solid particles released from a parent body such as a comet or asteroid, moving on similar orbits. Various ejection directions and velocities for individual meteoroids cause the width of a stream and the gradual distribution of meteoroids over the entire average orbit.

Metric ton : 1000 kilograms. A metric ton equals 2,204 pounds.

Metropolitan Area Network (MAN) : A network that covers an urban area – an extended local or a restricted wide area network.

Mev : Mega (million) electronvolt. A unit of energy used to describe the Total energy carried by a particle or photon.

MICR : Magnetic (ink) character recognition.

Microcomputer or Micro : A fairly small computer that is used by only one person at a time.

Microfiche : A rectangle of film, usually around 150 mm × 100 mm, carrying tiny photographic images of pages of text of drawings. A microfiche can hold between 60 and 300 pages, depending on the reduction.

Microfilm : A roll of film on to which tiny photographic images of pages of text or drawings are arranged in sequence.

Microfloppy : A floppy disc less than five inches (12.5 cm) across, generally between three and four inches.

Microform : General term for miniaturized storage of documents using a photographic process, e.g. microfiche and microfilm, with users needing a special projector to be able to read the documents.

Micrometeorite : A small extraterrestrial particle that has survived entry into the Earth's atmosphere. The actual size is not rigorously constrained but is operationally defined by the collection procedure. Micrometeorites found on the Earth's surface are smaller than 1mm, those collected in the Stratosphere are rarely as large as 50 micro-m.

A very small meteoroid with a diameter of less than a millimeter. Micrometeoroids form the bulk of the interplanetary solid matter scattered throughout the solar system.

Very small pieces of matter which are encountered in space.

Microphone : A sensor with a sound input and an electrical output.

Microprocessor : A computer processor on a single chip.

Microsecond : A millionth of a second.

Microviewdata : Local (or closed circuit) viewdata, even perhaps on a single micro.

Microwave : Electromagnetic radiation which has a long wavelength (between 1 mm and 30 cm). Microwaves can be used to study the Universe, communicate with satellites in orbit around Earth, and cook popcorn.

Microwave : Very short wavelength radio waves used in some telecommunications systems (and radar navigation, burglar alarms and ovens).

Microwave burst : A radiowave signal associated with optical and/or X-rayFlares.

Microwriter : A hand-held word processing device with its own system for coding characters using only five fingers of one hand.

Middle latitudes : With specific reference to zones of geomagnetic activity, "middle latitudes" refers to 20 deg. To 50 deg. Geomagnetic.

Milky Way Galaxy : Our home galaxy, the Milky Way is thought to be an average spiral galaxy. The Milky Way, a spiral galaxy, is the home of Earth, the Sun, and the rest of our solar system. The Milky Way contains more than 100 billion stars, has a diameter of 100,000 light-years, and belongs to the Local Group of galaxies. The Sun is about 28,000 light-years from the Milky Way's center in the Orion spiral arm.

Millibar : 1/1000 of a bar. Standard sea-level pressure is about 1013 millibars. This is 1/1000 of a bar; the standard sea-level pressure is about 1,013 millibars.

Minicomputer (Mini) : Cheaper and more compact than a mainframe, but more likely than a micro to have several users at once. It is becoming increasingly difficult to see a dividing line between the power, speed and memory of top range micros and bottom range minis.

Minor planets : Another term used for asteroids.

MIPS : Million instructions per second: a measure of the speed of a computer processor (see IPS).

Mix : In video production, a shot can be dissolved gradually into another by mixing the two: the proportion of the second shot increases as the first one fades. A mixer is a device for mixing two or more input signals in to a single output, as above or in a range of other ways.

MMI : Man/machine interface.

Mobile Switching Centre (MSC) : The equivalent of an exchange in a mobile (cellular) telephone system, handling the calls of a number of base stations.

Mobile Telephone : An instrument that can be carried around and used in different places, either within a small area (cordless telephone) or throughout a cellular network. The data transfers in each case involve radio.

Modem : Modulator/Demodulator: a device that allows digital devices like computers to transfer information to and from an analogue system. Modems can be built into computers or connected to them separately. An acoustic coupler is a modem.

Modular : A module is a self-contained unit that can readily be added to or built on. Computer hardware, telephone systems and programme sections are all modular in this sense.

Modulation : The encoding of an information signal on to a carrier by changing the carrier in some way. For instance, amplitude modulation (AM) depends on changing the size of the carrier; frequency modulation (FM) works by varying its frequency.

Molecular Cloud : A relatively dense, cold region of interstellar matter where hydrogen gas is primarily in molecular form. Stars generally form in molecular clouds. Molecular clouds appear as dark blotches in the sky because they block all the light behind them.

Molecular Velocity : The average speed of the molecules in a gas of a given temperature.

Molecule : A tightly knit group of two or more atoms bound together by electromagnetic forces among the atoms' electrons and nuclei. For example, water (H_2O) is two hydrogen atoms bound with one oxygen atom. Identical molecules have identical chemical properties.

Molecules in the interstellar medium : The interstellar gas can be studied at long wavelengths in the radio part of the spectrum. This reveals clouds of cool (20K) gas and dense (10**12 particles per cubic meter). Such clouds contain molecules and emit radiation at wavelengths characteristic of the molecules and their energies much as atoms do. Approximately 60 different species of molecules have been identified, some of them quite complex (involving as many as 10 atoms). It is believed that the survival of such molecules is made possible by the presence of dust which is able to shield them from the UV and X-rays of hot stars which would dissociate them.

Monitor : A high quality display screen giving a steadier clearer display than a television set; a type of operating software.

Monochrome : One colour only, as with a black and white television set or an amber or green monitor.

Mons : Mountain (plural: montes)

Moon : A large body orbiting a planet. On Earth's only moon, scientists have not detected life, water, or oxygen on this heavily cratered body. The Moon orbits our planet in about 28 days. With a diameter of 3500 km, Earth's Moon is actually quite large for a moon.

It orbits the Earth at a distance of 385,000 km. Since the same side of the moon always faces Earth, a Moon 'day' is 29.5 Earth days. It is thought that when the Earth formed it had no moon. Then, about 4.5 billion years ago a small planet hit Earth. The impact caused the Earth's surface to become molten, and the small planet became gravitationally bound to Earth, becoming the Moon.

Mount wilson magnetic classifications : Alpha. Denotes a unipolar sunspot group. Beta. A sunspot group having both positive and negative mag-Netic polarities, with a simple and distinct division between the polarities. Beta-Gamma. A sunspot group that is bipolar but in which no Continuous line can be drawn separating spots of opposite Polarities. Delta. A complex magnetic configuration of a solar sunspot Group consisting of opposite polarity umbrae within the same penumbra. Gamma. A complex active region in which the positive and nega-live polarities are so irregularly distributed as to prevent Classification as a bipolar group.

Mouse : An input device roughly the size of a pack of cards, which the user rolls around on a desk top to control the movement of a pointer on a screen. Action choices are made by pressing buttons on the mouse.

mp/m : A multi-user operating system derived from cp/m.

MSC : Mobile switching centre.

MS-DOS : A 16-bit operating system first commissioned by IBM for its Personal Computer (on which it is known as Pc-DOS) but available on many other machines, its main rival is cp/m-86.

Multi-Access : Multi-user.

Multi-Addressing : Such a technique allows a given message to be sent (by telex, for instance) to a number of different addresses.

Multi-Layer Insulation (MLI) : A "skin" or blanket of insulation covering the Hubble Space Telescope, which protects the observatory from temperature extremes. This insulation protects the telescope from the cold of outer space and also reflects sunlight so that the telescope does not become too warm. The MLI on Hubble is made up of many layers of aluminized Kapton, with an outer layer of aluminized Teflon.

Multiplexer (MUX) : A device allowing more than one signal at a time to be transmitted through a single channel. One method is to split up the frequency band available into several narrow bands and allocate one to each source; this is frequency division multiplexing (FDM). Another is to allocate the whole channel to several sources in turn by dividing up each second into short slots; time division multiplexing (TDM).

Multi-Programming : A system, offered by some operating software to make processor usage more efficient, which runs more than one programme during a given period by switching attention between them from moment to moment.

Multistream : A British Telecom service which gives access to the PSS at local call rates by use of the same telephone number in all parts of the country.

Multi-Tasking : Describes a 'concurrent' system – one that can deal with two or more programmes at a time.

Multi-User : Describes a system that can work with more than one user at a time.

Mutation : A change in genes from normal to abnormal, occurring for various reasons, that can be passed from generation to generation.

Mux : Multiplexer.

MYLAR : A tough polyester material used as an insulator.

❑❑❑

N

Nano : Prefix for a thousand millionth, as in nanosecond, 10^{-9} second

Nanotesla (nt) : A unit of magnetism 10.0E-09 tesla, equivalent to a gamma (10.0E-05 gauss).

Narrowband : General term for a communication channel with restricted bandwidth and thus limited capacity for information transfer, sometimes used for channels restricted to 300 Hz, and sometimes extended to those able to carry telephone conversations (up to 3000 Hz or more) (contrast broadband).

Narrowcast : The transmission of signals intended for a specific and relatively small audience, using cable, satellite or radio waves, likely to be financed differently from broadcasting, perhaps by subscription and/or by charges related to connection time.

NASA : The National Aeronautics and Space Administration which oversees the space program in the United States.

National Aeronautics And Space Administration (NASA) **:** A Federal agency created on July 29, 1958 after President Dwight Eisenhower signed the National Aeronautics and Space Act of 1958. NASA coordinates space exploration efforts as well as traditional aeronautical research functions.

Near Infrared Camera And Multi-Object Spectrometer (NICMOS) **:** An instrument that sees objects in near-infrared wavelengths, which are slightly longer than the wavelengths of visible light. (Human eyes cannot see infrared light.) NICMOS is actually three cameras in one, each with different fields of view. Many secrets about the birth of stars, solar systems, and galaxies are revealed in infrared light, which can penetrate the interstellar gas and dust that blocks visible light. In addition, light from the most distant objects in the universe "shifts" into infrared wavelengths due to the universe's expansion. By studying objects and phenomena in this spectral region, astronomers probe our universe's past, present, and future; and learn how galaxies, stars, and planetary systems form. Astronauts installed NICMOS aboard the Hubble Space Telescope in February 1997 during the Second Servicing Mission.

Near-Infrared : The region of the infrared spectrum that is closest to visible light. Near-infrared light has slightly longer wavelengths and slightly lower frequencies and energies than visible light.

Nebula : A cloud of interstellar gas and dust. A cloud of interstellar gas. One of the most famous nebula is the Great Orion Nebula, which can be seen with the unaided eye. It is the middle 'star' of the sword of Orion. A low density cloud of gas and dust in which a star is born.

Nebular Theory : The idea that our solar system originated in a contracting, rotating cloud of gas that flattened to form a disk as it contracted. According to this theory, the Sun formed at the center of the disk and the planets formed in concentric bands of the disk.

Neptune : The eighth planet and the most distant giant gaseous planet in our solar system. The planet is 30 times the Earth's distance from the Sun, and each orbit takes 165 Earth years. Neptune is the fourth largest planet and has at least eight moons, the largest of which is Triton. Neptune has a ring system, just like all the giant gaseous outer planets.

Network : System for linking one or more computers and terminals so that they can communicate with each other and share facilities like disc drives and printers (see also local area network, metropolitan area network and wide area network).

Neujmin : Giopgoriy N. Ukrainian astronomer; discovered the asteroid 951 Gaspra.

Neutral line : The line that separates longitudinal magnetic fields of opposite polarity.

Neutrino : A class of elementary particle thought to have either no mass or very little mass. If neutrinos have any mass, then they may account for some fraction of dark matter. For more on neutrinos, check out this big bang cosmology primer.

A fundamental particle supposedly produced in massive numbers by the nuclear reactions in stars. They are very hard to detect since the vast majority of them pass completely through the Earth without interacting.

A neutral, weakly interacting elementary particle having a very tiny mass. Stars like the Sun produce more than 200 trillion trillion trillion neutrinos every second. Neutrinos from the Sun interact so weakly with other matter that they pass straight through the Earth as if it weren't there.

Any of three species of very weakly-interacting lepton with an extremely small, possibly zero, mass. Electron neutrinos are generated in the interior of the Sun (and other stars). Generally such neutrinos do not interact with matter and stream out through the Sun. A very few of these many neutrinos can be detected in sophisticated detectors here on Earth, giving us a "window" into the interior of the Sun. In 1987 neutrinos from a Supernova in the Large Magellanic Cloud were detected in terrestrial neutrino experiments.

Neutrino Detector : A device designed to detect neutrinos.

Neutron : A charge-neutral particle (of the hadron type) which is one of the two particles that make up the nuclei of atoms. Neutrons are unstable outside the nucleus, but stable within it. The number of protons in the nucleus determines what element that nucleus is. Different isotopes of a given element have different numbers of neutrons in the nucleus. The total number of neutrons and protons affects properties such as radioactivity or stability, the types of nuclear reactions, if any, in which the isotope will participate, and so forth.

A neutral (no electric charge) elementary particle having slightly more mass than a proton and residing in the nucleus of all atoms other than hydrogen.

A sub-atomic particle found in the nuclei of an atom. Unlike the proton and electron, the neutron has no net charge.

Neutron Degeneracy Pressure : Quantum mechanics restricts the number of neutrons that can have low energy. Each neutron must occupy its own energy state. When neutrons are packed together, as they are in a neutron star, the number of available low energy states is too small and many neutrons are forced into high energy states. These high energy neutrons make up the entire pressure supporting the neutron star. Because the pressure arises from this quantum mechanical effect, it is insensitive to temperature, i.e., the pressure doesn't go down as the star cools. Similar to electron degeneracy pressure but, because the neutron is much more massive than the electron, neutron degeneracy pressure is much larger and can support stars more massive than the Chandrasekhar mass limit.

Neutron Star : A dead "star" supported by neutron degeneracy pressure. A neutron star is the core remnant left over after a supernova explosion.

An extremely compact ball of neutrons created from the central core of a star that collapsed under gravity during a supernova explosion. Neutron stars are extremely dense: they are only 10 kilometers or so in size, but have the mass of an average star (usually about 1.5 times more massive than our Sun). A neutron star that regularly emits pulses of radiation is known as a pulsar.

Such objects typically produce synchrotron radiation beams which, if the orientation is right, can flash across the Earth to be seen as the "pulsar" phenomenon first discovered by Jocelyn Bell in 1967.

Newton, Isaac 1642-1727 **:** English cleric and scientist; discovered the classical laws of motion and gravity; the bit with the apple is probably apocryphal.

Nexus : A point in a system, such as a network at which there are inter-connections.

Nibble : Half a byte – a group of four bits.

Nicholson, Seth Barnes 1891-1963 **:** American astronomer; discovered Lysithea, Ananke, Carme and Sinope; also did important work on sunspots.

Node : A junction or data forwarding point on a network (also called switch in the former case).

Noise : Unwanted fluctuations that occur in the output of any electronic device. It can be associated with background radiation and thermal radiation from your instrument.

Non-Thermal Radiation : Radiation that is not produced from heat energy — for example, radiation released when a very fast-moving charged particle (such as an electron) interacts with a magnetic force field. Because the electron's velocity in this case is not related to the gas temperature, this process has nothing to do with heat.

Normalization : Actions taken to make a medical experience or setting as comfortable, normal, and familiar as possible, which help children feel more secure and in control.

North Celestial Pole (NCP) **:** A direction determined by the projection of the Earth's North Pole onto the celestial sphere. It corresponds to a declination of +90 degrees. The North Star, Polaris, sits roughly at the NCP.

Nova : A white dwarf in a binary system, that is not near the 1.4 solar mass limit, can gain mass from a expanding companion. As this mass accumulates, fusion of its hydrogen can be triggered. This causes the mass to be blown off in a nova explosion, while leaving the white dwarf unaffected. Such explosions can occur periodically on time scales of around 75 years or longer. The pattern of suddenly increasing brightness followed by a gradual decline over a period of months is similar to that of a supernova, but the energies are many orders of magnitude lower.

A binary star system (consisting of a white dwarf and a companion star) that rapidly brightens, then slowly fades back to normal.

A star that experiences an abrupt increase in brightness by a factor of a million (in contrast to the much brighter supernova). A nova is produced in a semidetached binary system where hydrogen-rich matter is being transferred onto a white dwarf. As more and more hydrogen builds up on the surface the temperature rises. The material is degenerate so when the temperature becomes high enough for nuclear burning to take place it does so explosively producing a nova.

NTSC : The video colour standard, established in the US, that applies to systems that handle colour in a certain way and use a 525-line screen running at 30 frames (60 fields) a second. Used throughout North America and Japan.

Nuclear fusion : A nuclear process whereby several small nuclei are combined to make a larger one whose mass is slightly smaller than the sum of the small ones. The difference in mass is converted to energy by Einstein's famous equivalence E=mc2. This is the source of the Sun's energy therefore ultimately of (almost) all energy on Earth.

Nuclear magnitude : See definition for m_2, above.

Nuclear Transformation : The process by which an atomic nucleus is transformed into another type of atomic nucleus. For example, by removing an alpha particle from the nucleus, the element radium is transformed into the element radon.

Nuclei : The core of an atom, the nuclei consists of various numbers of protons and neutrons, depending upon the element.

Nucleosynthesis : The process by which nuclear reactions produce the various elements of the periodic table.

Nucleus, Galactic : The central region of a galaxy characterized by high densities of stars. The nucleus may also contain a supermassive black hole and may be the source of considerable high-energy, nonstellar luminosity.

Numeric : Describes data that consists of numbers only (compare with alphanumeric).

Nutation : The short-period oscillations in the motion of the pole of rotation of a freely rotating body that is undergoing torque from external gravitational forces. Nutation of the Earth's pole is discussed in terms of components in obliquity and longitude. [1]

Nybble : Alternative for nibble.

O

Obliquity : The angle between the equatorial and orbital planes (or the rotational and orbital poles) of a body. The obliquity of the ecliptic for the Earth is the angle between the equatorial and ecliptic planes. [1]

Observable Universe : The portion of the entire universe that can be seen from Earth.

Occultation : The blockage of light by the intervention of another object; a planet can occult (block) the light from a distant star.

This has nothing to do with Satan worship. The word is derived from a Latin word meaning "hiding." This occurs when a planet passes between Earth and a star. We can more easily detect faint asteroids and outer planets by knowing when they'll pass close to an easy-to-find star.

Oceanus : Literally "ocean"; really a large circular plain

Octet : A group of eight bits, normally the same as a byte.

ODA : Office documentation architecture: a set of standards that allow the exchange of documents in electronic form between IT systems.

Office of the Future : The shorthand term for a networked computer based office with little call on paper, but using electronic systems for all its word and information processing, analysis, storage and communication purposes.

Offline : Describes a hardware device that is not at the moment linked to a computer but is resting or carrying out its own processing locally.

Offset (Litho) : A simple but effective printing system, cheap enough to be within reach of even quite small firms.

Oftel : The Office of Telecommunications, the British regulatory body for this field.

Old : A planetary surface that has been modified little since its formation typically featuring large numbers of impact craters (compare young).

Omega : The ratio of the actual density of the universe to the critical density. A value greater than one indicates that the universe is denser than the critical value and this corresponds to a closed universe. A value less than one is an open universe. The ratio of the observed density of the Universe to the critical density of the Universe is given by the Greek letter omega. If omega is less than one the Universe will continue expanding until it is so large that it dies a cold death. If omega equals one the Universe will eventually stop expanding but will not collapse; the Universe will die a cold static death. If omega is greater than one, then the Universe will die a hot, fiery death in a Big Crunch. For theoretical reasons, cosmologists believe that omega = 1. For more about omega check out the big bang cosmology primer.

Online : Connected to a working computer system, remotely through a standard telephone link or locally.

Oort cloud : A huge cloud which is thought to surround our solar system and reach over halfway to the nearest star. Comets originate in the Oort Cloud.

A vast spherical region in the outer reaches of our solar system where a trillion long-period comets (those with orbital periods greater than 200 years) reside. Comets from the Oort Cloud come from all directions, often from as far away as 50,000 astronomical units.

Oort, Jan Hendrik 1900-1992 **:** Dutch astronomer made major contributions to knowledge of the structure and rotation of our galaxy. More or less as a sideline, Oort studied comets as well. The result of this work was a theory, now widely accepted, that the Sun is surrounded by a distant cloud of comet-stuff, now called the Oort cloud, bits of which are occasionally hurled into the solar system as comets.

Opacity : The degree to which light is prevented from passing through an object or a substance. Opacity is the opposite of transparency. As an object's opacity increases, the amount of light passing through it decreases. Glass, for example, is transparent and most clouds are opaque.

The property of a substance that determines how hard it is for radiation to get through that substance (hence how "opaque" that substance is). The atmosphere has low opacity to light. Fog has a much higher opacity and light cannot stream through a fog very far before being scattered. The opacity of a substance determines how well radiation can transport heat by radiative transport.

Open Cluster : Also known as a galactic cluster, an open cluster consists of numerous young stars that formed at the same time within a large cloud of interstellar dust and gas. Open clusters are located in the spiral arms or the disks of galaxies. The Pleiades is an example of an open cluster.

An open cluster is a somewhat loose, irregular grouping of several hundred stars, around 10 pc across and generally found in the disk of the Galaxy. Open clusters consist of Population I stars and represent stars formed relatively recently at about the same time. Examples include the Pleiades and the Hyades.

Open Systems Interconnection (OSI) : Protocols for the exchange of data between different IT systems.

Open Universe : 1. A geometrical model of the universe in which the overall structure of the universe extends infinitely in all directions. The rules of geometry in an open universe are like those that would apply on a saddle-shaped surface. 2. A model of the universe which expands forever and is infinite in space and time, although it begins with a Big Bang. The total mass density of the universe is too small to cause recollapse.

Operating Environment : A comprehensive operating system complete with integrated software and special hardware.

Operating Software (OS) : A vital programme (or suite) in overall control of a computer whenever it is operating. Without the OS, the computer could not handle programmes, process data, retrieve from disc or send output to a printer; it would be useless. Modern computers often have resident operating systems on ROM chips, others load it from disc as needed. Many 16-bit micros give the user a choice of operating system. The characteristics of the OS determine how the user perceives the computer and how easy it is to use.

Operator : A person with the task of keeping a large computer system running smoothly.

Opposition : A superior planet is said to be "in opposition" when it is directly on the opposite side of the Earth from the Sun. This is generally the closest it comes to the Earth and the time at which it is most easily visible.

The closest approach of an object in our solar system (usually a planet) to Earth during the course of a year. Due to the nature of orbital mechanics, this is always when the object is in the opposite direction of the sun. Therefore, objects in opposition will always be visible throughout the night.

Optical : To do with light. Light waves have very high frequencies compared with radio waves, giving far greater bandwidth and information carrying capacity. The optical fibres that can carry them are very important in modern telecommunications. Some video disc systems are optical as well – they depend on the reflection or transmission of laser light. So too are compact discs.

Optical Character Recognition (OCR) : Automatic recognition by machine of characters based on their shapes.

Optical Depth : 1. A measure of the absorption of radiation as it passes through a medium. Essentially, it is how far light can penetrate a material. For example, dirty, muddy water has a shorter optical depth than clear water. 2. Optical depth is a measure of the transparency of a ring system. When a ring is "optically thick" (i.e., the optical depth is large), the ring is nearly opaque and very little light passes through. When a ring is "optically thin" (i.e., the optical depth is small), very little material is present and most of the light passes through.

Optical Fibre : A flexible strand of highly pure glass drawn out to be finer than a human hair. Compared with traditional metal communication cables, optical fibres are very light and fine, and have a much higher bandwidth.

Optical Mark Reader (OMR) : A device for reading pencil marks made in certain positions on a special form.

Optical Publishing : Publishing material in optical form, i.e. on video disc or compact disc in particular.

Optical ROM (OROM) : A video disc used as a computer's read-only backing store.

Optical Telescope : A telescope that gathers and magnifies visible light. The two basic types of optical telescopes are refracting (using lenses) and reflecting (using mirrors). The Hubble Space Telescope is an example of a reflecting telescope.

Oracle : The teletext service provided by the Independent Broadcasting Authority in Britain.

Orbit : The path followed by a celestial body.

A specific path followed by a planet, satellite, etc.

The path a planet travels around the Sun; the path of any heavenly body around another heavenly body; for example, the path of a moon around a planet.

The path of an object that is moving around a second object or point.

The path of one object about another (used here for an object orbiting the sun).

Orbital elements : Parameters (numbers) that determine an object's location and motion in its orbit about another object. In the case of solar-system objects such as comets and planets, one must ultimately account for perturbing gravitational effects of numerous other planets in the solar system (not merely the sun), and when such account is made, one has what are called "osculating elements" (which are always changing with time and which therefore must have a stated epoch of validity). Six elements are usually used to determine uniquely the orbit of an object in orbit about the sun, with a seventh element (the epoch, or time, for which the elements are valid) added when planetary perturbations are allowed for; initial ("preliminary") orbit determinations shortly after the discovery of a new comet or minor planet (when very few observations are available) are usually "two-body determinations", meaning that only the object and the sun are taken into account — with, of course, the earth in terms of observing perspective) work with only the following six orbital elements: time of perihelion passage (T) [sometimes taken instead as an angular measure called "mean anomaly", M]; perihelion distance (q), usually given in AU; eccentricity (e) of the orbit; and three angles (for which the mean equinox must be specified) — the argument of perihelion (lower-case Greek letter omega), the longitude of the ascending node (upper-case Greek letter Omega), and the inclination (i) of the orbit with respect to the ecliptic.

Orbital Period : The time required for an object to make a complete revolution along its orbit. For example, the orbital period for a typical main-belt asteroid is about 4 years.

Organizer : A type of business software with such features as diary, address book and appointments database.

OROM : Optical ROM.

OSI : Open systems interconnection.

Output : Any result which comes from a system, usually in the form of text and graphics displayed on a screen and/or printed on paper.

Overwrite : To record on top of; in word processing, a mode in which characters entered replace what is there already.

Ozone Layer : A region in the upper atmosphere that has high concentrations of ozone (triatomic oxygen, 0_3). The ozone layer protects the Earth by absorbing the Sun's high-energy ultraviolet radiation.

P

PABX : Old acronym for private (automatic) branch exchange, PBX.

Package : Programme or set of programmes complete with documentation, designed for a particular application.

Packet Assembly and Disassembly Point (PAD) : A node in a PSS at which the packets that form a complete message from a sender are made up from that message, or re-joined to go to the receiver.

Packet Switching : A method of transmitting information involving splitting a message into units, each of standard size (maybe half a kilobyte) and format and labelled with source and destination. The packets then each transfer by the route that makes most efficient use of the network concerned; the system reassembles them into the original message at the other end. Very short messages go in a single packet and therefore pass through the system more quickly (contrast circuit switching; see also message switching and the last entry).

PAD : Packet assembly and disassembly point: unit of information in a viewdata system with a unique page number to allow routeing and direct access. It may, however, consist of a linked sequence of single frames (screensful).

Paddle : Joystick.

Page Printer : A fast, quiet printer in effect producing output a page at a time, the laser printer being a common type. It is rather like a photocopier with an electronic input.

Pahoehoe : A type of basalt lava flow characterized by a smooth glassy skin, and constructed of innumerable "flow units" called "toes"; pahoehoe flows advance at rates of 1 to 10 meters (3 to 33 feet) hour and are associated with low-effusion-rate eruptions with little to no fountaining.

PAL : Phase alternating line: colour video standard.

Paleozoic : A geological term denoting the time in Earth history between 570 and 245 million years ago.

Palimpsest : A circular feature on the surface of dark icy moons such as Ganymede and Callisto lacking the relief associated with craters; Pamlimpsests are thought to be impact craters where the topographic relief of the crater has been eliminated by slow adjustment of the icy surface.

Palus : Literally "swamp"; really a small plain

Paperless Office : Another name for the office of the future.

Parallax : Generally speaking, parallax is the apparent shift in the direction to an object as seen from two different locations. This shift can be used to determine distances (through "triangulation"). Stellar parallax occurs as the Earth orbits the Sun and our line of sight to a nearby star varies. The effect is to make the star appear to shift position over the course of the year. In reality, stellar distances are so great that parallax shifts are less than an arc second, completely unobservable to the unaided eye.

The apparent shift of an object's position when viewed from different locations. Parallax, also called trigonometric parallax, is used to determine the distance to nearby stars. As the Earth's position changes during its yearly orbit around the Sun, the apparent locations of nearby stars slightly shift. The stars' distances can be calculated from those slight shifts with basic trigonometric methods.

Parallel Interface : A connection between two devices that is capable of parallel data handling, i.e. passing information more than one bit at a time.

Parity Check : A method of checking data for simple input or handling errors.

Parsec (pc) : A astronomical distance approximately 3.3 light years. The term parsec comes from a **par**allax **sec**ond, since a parsec is defined by the parallax of object as seen from opposite ends of the Earth's orbit.

A useful unit for measuring the distances between astronomical objects, equal to 3.26 light-years and 3.085678 * 10^{13} kilometers, or approximately 18 trillion miles. A parsec is also equivalent to 103,132 trips to the Sun and back. 206265 AU = 3.26 light year.

A unit of **distance** used to describe the vast scales of the cosmos, the parsec is equal to about 3.262 lightyears, or 3.09×10^{16} meters. A star that is one parsec away would produce a parallax angle of one second of arc. A star that has a parallax shift of 0.1 arcseconds would be at a distance of 10 parsecs, and so forth. One parsec equals 3.26 light-years.

Particle Accelerators : A huge device used by particle physicists to accelerate particles. By accelerating particles, scientists can better understand particle interactions.

Particle Physics : The study of elementary particle interactions. Particle physicists historically have worked at particle accelerators. Recently particle physicists have worked with astrophysicists to try to understand stars and other stellar objects.

Password : These secret codes are to prevent unauthorized use of a system. Passwords can give different categories of user access to different levels of privileged information.

Patera : Shallow crater; scalloped, complex edge.

Payload bay : The main body of the Space Shuttle where the payload, or cargo, is stored.

Payroll : The name for programmes that work out a firm's wages and salaries, print the pay slips, and prepare for payment.

PBX : Private branch exchange.

PC : Personal computer.

PCB : Printed circuit board.

PCM : Pulse code modulation.

Peak ring : A central uplift characterized by a ring of peaks rather than a single peak; peak rings are typical of larger terrestrial craters above about 50 kilometers (30 miles) in diameter.

Peculiar Velocity : Any velocity a galaxy has with respect to us that is not a Hubble law velocity due to the expansion of space. Peculiar velocities are due to the gravitaional influences of nearby galaxies, for example, if a galaxy is orbiting in a cluster of galaxies. Peculiar velocites add or subtract an additional component to the observed redshift, confusing somewhat the determination of the Hubble constant.

PEL : The same as pixel, but used in the context of fax.

Penumbra : Literally, "dim light"; the outer filamentary region of a sunspot. The sunspot area that may surround the darker umbra or umbrae. It Consists of linear bright and dark elements radial from the sunspot Umbra.

Perigee : The closest approach of a planet or moon to the star or planet that it's orbiting.

The point where (and when) an object's orbit *about the earth* in which it is closest to the earth; only applicable to objects orbiting the earth (not to objects orbiting the sun — a common error).

The point in its orbit where a planet is closest to the Sun. When referring to objects orbiting the Earth the term **perigee** is used; the term **periapsis** is used for orbits around other bodies. (opposite of aphelion)

Perihelion Distance : The distance between the orbiting body and the sun at it's closest approach.

abbr. Q, distance of the least heliocentric separation for a body in an eccentric orbit; q=a(1-e).

Periodic Comet : A comet in a closed, elliptical orbit within our solar system. These comets typically have orbital periods of less than 200 years. Many comets have orbits that keep them in the inner solar system and allow their trajectories to be calculated with great accuracy and precision. Perhaps the best-known periodic comet is Halley's comet, whose orbital period is 76 years.

Periodic Table (of the Elements) **:** A chart of all the known chemical elements arranged according to the number of protons in the nucleus (also known as the atomic number). Elements with similar properties are grouped together in the same column.

Period-Luminosity Law : A relationship that describes how the luminosity or absolute brightness of a Cepheid variable star depends on the period of time over which that brightness varies.

Period-Luminosity Relation : A relationship between the pulsation period of a variable star (e.g. A Cepheid) and its luminosity (or absolute magnitude). Generally the more luminous the star the longer the pulsation period. The relationship permits distances to be measured. One determineds the pulsation period and uses the relationship to get the absolute magnitude. The apparent magnitude of the star then gives you the distance modulus.

Peripheral : Any computer hardware other than the processor an input/output device or backing store in particular.

Perrine, Charles Dillon 1867-1951 **:** Argentine-American astronomer who discovered Himalia and Elara.

Persistence : Continuation of existing conditions. When a physical parameter Varies slowly, the best prediction is often persistence.

Persistence of Vision : The inability of our eyes to follow very rapid changes in what we see. Thus a light that flashes rapidly enough – more than about 40 times a second – will appear steady. This is the effect on which TV and movies depend.

Persistent train : Remaining glow due to ionization in the upper atmosphere after the passage of a meteoroid. The intensity and duration depend on the meteoroid's atmospheric entry velocity, its size, and its composition. Bright fireballs occasionally caused trains visible for several minutes.

Personal Computer : A computer that is small enough or cheap enough to be used mainly by one person.

Perturb : To cause a planet or satellite to deviate from a theoretically regular orbital motion .

Perturbations : Gravitational influences ("tugging" and "pulling") of one astronomical body on another. Comets are strongly perturbed by the gravitational forces of the major planets, particularly by the largest planet, Jupiter. These perturbations must be allowed for in orbit computations, and they lead to what are known as "osculating elements" (which means that the orbital element numbers change from day to day and month to month due to continued perturbations by the major planets, so that an epoch is necessarily stated to denote the particular date that the elements are valid.

Phase angle : For a solar system object besides the earth and sun, the angle between the earth and the sun (or the earth's elongation from the sun) as seen from that third object. The phase angle is given in ephemerides on *IAU Circulars* and *Minor Planet Circulars* is denoted by either of the lower-case Greek letters beta or phi.

Photo-Cell : A sensor with optical input and electrical output.

Photodisintegration : The process by which atomic nuclei are broken apart into their constituent protons and neutrons by the impact of high energy gamma rays (photons). Photodisintegration takes place during the core collapse phase of a Type II supernova explosion.

Photoelectric Effect : There is a phenomenon called the photoelectric effect wherein light incident upon certain metals can cause currents to flow (this is the basis of photocells). What happens is that the light causes electrons to be knocked loose from the surface. However certain experimental data was difficult to explain using the standard wave picture of light: The light had to be above a certain threshold frequency or no current would flow, regardless of the intensity. The release of electrons from a solid material when it is struck by radiant energy, such as visible or ultraviolet light, X-rays, or gamma rays.

Photographic observations : The meteors are captured on a photographic film or plate. The accuracy of the derived meteor coordinates is very high. Normal-lens photography is restricted to meteors brighter than about +1mag. Multiple-station photography allows the determination of precise meteoroid orbits.

Photometer : An instrument that measures the intensity of light. Astronomers use photometers to measure the brightness of celestial objects.

Photometry : The measurement of light. Specifically refers to the procedure of highly accurate measuring of the apparent magnitudes of astronomical objects. In general, astronomers measure only a portion of the wavelength spectrum when they do photometry. Different types of photometry are defined by the portion of the wavelength that they examine. For example "UBV Photometry" measures the light within three standard regions defined by filters. These are Ultraviolet, Blue and Visual (hence UBV). There are many different photometry systems and standards.

In astronomy, the measurement of the light emitting from astronomical objects, generally in the visible or infrared bands, in which a specific or general wavelength band is normally specified.

Photon : A packet of electromagnetic energy, such as light. A photon is regarded as a charge-less, mass-less particle having an indefinitely long lifetime.

Experiments have shown that light of a given energy (frequency) is not something that can be broken up indefinitely. Rather for a given frequency it comes in discrete bundles with energy hf where h is

Planck's constant and f is the frequency. These discrete bundles of light are known as photons. It is often useful to think of light as a bunch of particle photons. Other times it is useful to think of light as a wave. Astronomers do both as needed.

Photosphere : The extremely thin, visible surface layer of the Sun or a star. The average temperature of the Sun's photosphere is about 5800 Kelvin (about 10,000° F). Although the Sun is completely made up of gas, its gas is so dense that we cannot see through it. When we look at the Sun, we are seeing the photosphere.

The lowest layer of the solar atmosphere; corresponds to the Solar surface viewed in WHITE LIGHT. Sunspots and faculae are Observed in the photosphere.

The surface layer of the sun where the continuous blackbody-type spectrum is produced that we directly observe when we look at the Sun. The Sun doesn't have a "surface" like we usually think of one, since it is a ball of gas, but the photosphere looks like a surface because it is the point where light from the hot gas of the Sun escapes into space without further scattering. It is as far into the Sun as we can directly see.

The visible surface of the Sun; the upper surface of a convecting layer of gases in the outer portion of the sun whose temperature causes it to radiate light at visible wavelengths; sunspots and faculae are observed in the photosphere.

Photosynthesis : The process by which plants use carbon dioxide, nutrients, and sunlight to produce food.

Photo-Typesetter : A processor-based system that prepares fully edited and laid out documents for printing, being rather like an advanced text and graphics processor (see also desktop publishing).

Phreatic eruption : A volcanic eruption or explosion of steam, mud or other material that is not incandescent; this form of eruption is caused by the heating and consequent expansion of ground water due to an adjacent igneous heat source.

Physicist : A person who studies physics.

Physics : The science of matter and energy, and of interactions between the two. A person who studies physics is called a physicist.

Piazzi, Giuseppe 1746-1826 : Astronomer, born in Ponte di Valtellina, Italy. He became a Theatine monk, professor of theology in Rome (1779), and professor of mathematics at the Academy of Palermo (1780). He set up an observatory at Palermo in 1789, published a star catalog (1803, 1814) and discovered and named the first minor planet, Ceres.

Pickering, William Henry 1858-1938 : American astronomer. His photographs of Mars, among the earliest obtained, provided a basis for his opposition to Lowell's observations of supposed canals on Mars. Discovered Phoebe.

Pickoff Mirror : One of four flat mirrors inside the Hubble Space Telescope. Each mirror is tilted at a 45-degree angle to the incoming light, diverting a small portion of it to the optical detectors or to one of the fine guidance sensors.

PIN : Personal identification number: a password to identify the user of a cash dispenser or computer system.

Pixel : A light-sensitive picture element on a charge-coupled device (CCD) or some other kind of digital camera. A pixel is a tiny cell that, placed together with other pixels, resembles the mesh on a screen door. The Hubble Space Telescope's Wide Field and Planetary Camera 2 has four ccds, each containing 640,000 pixels. Each pixel collects light from a celestial object and converts it into a number. The numbers (all 2,560,000 of them) are sent to ground-based computers, which convert them into an image. The greater number of pixels, the sharper the image.

Plage : An extended emission feature of an active region that exists from The emergence of the first magnetic flux until the widely scattered Remnant magnetic fields merge with the background.

Bright regions seen in the solar chromosphere.

Plage corridor : A space in chromospheric (see CHROMOSPHERE) PLAGE lacking

Plagenil : Spotless disc free of calcium plage

Plains : Vast, flat areas with low elevation.

Planar features : Microscopic features in grains of quartz or feldspar consisting of very narrow planes of glassy material arranged in parallel sets that have distinct orientations with respect to the grain's crystal structure.

Planck Curve : The graphical representation of the mathematical relationship between the frequency (or wavelength) and intensity of radiation emitted from an object by virtue of its heat energy.

Planet : An object orbiting a star that is not a brown dwarf but bigger than an asteroid. This is somewhat ambiguous. In our solar system it is really an historical definition which boils down to "a planet is a member of the set {Mercury, Venus, Earth, Mars, Jupiter, Saturn, Uranus, Neptune, Pluto}". All the known planets orbiting other stars are large gas planets so no ambiguity yet arises there. But when we begin to discover terrestrial planets and then smaller objects it will become necessary to make some further arbitrary definition.

An object that orbits a star. Although smaller than stars, planets are relatively large and shine only by reflected light. Planets are made up mostly of rock or gas, with a small, solid core. In our solar system, the inner planets — Mercury, Venus, Earth, and Mars — are the rocky objects, and most of the outer planets — Jupiter, Saturn, Uranus, and Neptune — are the gaseous ones. Because Pluto is made largely of ice, like a comet, some astronomers do not consider it a true planet.

Planetary Nebula : At the end of the life of a lower mass star it is on the asymptotic giant branch as a huge red giant. The core is composed of carbon and oxygen; helium burning has ceased. Helium Shell Flashes take place in the region around the core and their energy causes the outer layers to be ejected. The expanding ejected nebula composed of the dying star's outer envelope is called a planetary nebula. An expanding shell of glowing gas expelled by a star late in its life. Our Sun will create a planetary nebula at the end of its life.

Stars (like the Sun) which exhaust their sources of fusion energy move more or less horizontally to the left in the HR diagram before turning and dropping dramatically in luminosity as they cool. During this evolution, such stars can slough off shells of outer material. These shells appear in a telescope as greenish disks or as "smoke rings". Because of the former appearance, similar to that of the more distant planets, they were called planetary nebulae. These shells of gas dissipate slowly and there is evidence that new shells are released. 3. A type of nebula caused by an expanding cloud of gas ejected by a dying star. For cool pictures, check out HST's planetary nebula gallery.

Planetesimal : A small body of rock and/or ice — under 10 kilometers (6 miles) across — formed during the early stages of the solar system. Planetesimals are the building blocks of planets, but many never combined to form large bodies. Asteroids are one example of planetesimals.

Planets : Large bodies that orbit around stars. There are nine planets in our solar system. Planets are categorized into two types: gas giant planets, and terrestrial planets.

Planitia : Broad plains that occupy lowlands on planetary surfaces. Low plain.

Planum : A plateau or high plain.

Plasma : A low-density gas in which the individual atoms are charged, even though the total number of positive and negative charges is equal, maintaining an overall electrical neutrality.

A substance composed of charged particles, like ions and electrons, and possibly some neutral particles. Our Sun is made of plasma. Overall, the charge of a plasma is electrically neutral. Plasma is regarded as an additional state of matter because its properties are different from those of solids, liquids, and normal gases.

Any ionized gas, that is, any gas containing ions and electrons.

The fluid component of blood, which contains platelets, clotting factors, and other proteins.

The high- energy state of matter when electrons are ripped from molecules, leaving a mixture of the negatively charged electrons and the positively charged ions. It is formed at high temperatures.

Platelets (Platelet Plug) : Small cell fragments in the blood that attach to damaged blood vessels and quickly form a plug to prevent blood loss.

Play : Spontaneous and/or voluntary interactions and activities that are pleasurable and enjoyable; hands-on experiences that lead to learning/development of knowledge; opportunities to master activities through repetition and experimentation.

Plotter : An output device for drawing and lettering in which a computer controls the movement of one or more pens directly.

Plug Compatible : A device made by one manufacturer that can be plugged straight into something made by another, then working without any adjustments.

Pluto : The outermost planet in our solar system. Pluto is, on average, about 40 times the Earth's distance from the Sun. Pluto orbits the Sun in 248 Earth years.

The smallest planet in our solar system. Pluto is neither a gas giant planet, nor a terrestrial planet, but rather is though to have been gravitationally captured by our Sun.

Point of Sale (POS) : The place where a purchase transaction usually takes place, such as the checkout in a shop.

Pointer : A symbol on a WIMP screen under mouse control that lets the user point to the icon that represents a task to be done; a link in computer memory between two related data items.

Polar Cap Absorption (PCA) : An anomalous condition of the polar ionosphere whereby HF and VHF (3 - 300 mhz) radiowaves are absorbed, and LF And VLF (3 - 300 khz) radiowaves are reflected at lower altitudes Than normal. In practice, the absorption is inferred from the Proton flux at energies greater than 10 mev, so that pcas and proton events are simultaneous. Transpolar radio paths may still be disturbed for days, up to weeks, following the end of a proton event.

Polaris : The proper name of the north star.

Polarization : A special property of light; light has three properties, brightness, color and polarization.

Polarization of starlight : In addition to their wavelength, photons exhibit a direction of their vibration plane, This is called polarization when many individual photons share a common direction. Observations of the polarization of sources at various wavelengths can reveal information about the interstellar dust and the strength and direction of the magnetic fields in the Galaxy.

Polling : A technique whereby a processor continually checks the channels to its peripherals to see if there is data to be transferred. Automatic polling can also be carried out by some terminals, in telex for instance, to see if there are messages at other terminals.

Pope, Alexander 1688-1744 : English writer best remembered for his satirical mock-epic poems *The Rape of the Lock* and *The Dunciad*.

Population I Stars : Relatively young stars, containing a larger fraction of metals, found mainly in the disk of the Galaxy.

Population II Stars : Relatively old stars, containing a smaller fraction of metals, found mainly in the halo of the Galaxy and in Globular Clusters.

Port : A device surgically implanted under the chest wall that allows for factor infusions without having to locate an accessible vein.

Portable : Easy to carry, like a small microcomputer also capable of running on other equipment, like a standard cp/m programme.

POS : Point of sale.

Post-flare loops : a loop prominence system often seen after a major two-ribbon flare, which bridges the ribbons.

Potential Energy : The energy of an object owing to its position in a force field or its internal condition, as opposed to kinetic energy, which depends on its motion. Examples of objects with potential energy include a diver on a diving board and a coiled spring.

Power Line Transfer : A system which allows data transfers to pass through the normal electric mains wiring of a building or the power lines of the grid.

Poynting-Robertson effect : A dissipative force due to the anisotropic loss of momentum by a particle through re-radiation of solar energy. This causes aphelion collaps such that a circular orbit is soon attained; thereafter the particle spirals slowly towards the Sun. Small particles (below 1cm) are most severely affected because the force varies as the reciprocal of its size.

Precambrian : A geological term denoting the time in Earth history prior to 570 million years ago.

Precession : A slow but relatively uniform motion of the earth's rotational axis that causes changes in the coordinate systems used for mapping the sky. The earth's axis of rotation does not always point in the same direction, due to gravitational tugs by the sun and moon (known as lunisolar precession) and by the major planets (known as planetary precession).

Preparation for Medical Experience : Communication of accurate, developmentally appropriate information in advance of the experience, including the reason(s) for threatening or painful procedures, the anticipated sequence of events, and the sensations that will accompany the experience. Also, opportunities to physically interact with and discuss medical equipment and procedures.

Pressure ridge : A ridge formed by the uplift of a lava flow crust due to pressure of the flowing lava.

Prestel : A British public viewdata system which contains vast amounts of information in page format. Subscribers can order goods and catalogues as well as getting up-to-date information and sending electronic mail and telex messages. Prestel subscribers with micros need only a modem and communications software to be able to access, save and print Presetel frames.

Primary Mirror : A large mirror in a reflecting telescope that captures light from celestial objects and focuses it toward a smaller secondary mirror. The primary mirror in the Hubble Space Telescope measures 94.5 inches (2.4 meters) in diameter.

Prime Focus : The location where light reflected from the primary mirror of a reflecting telescope comes into focus. Placing a secondary mirror in the light path allows the light to be focused elsewhere, in a more convenient location for the science instruments.

Primordial Nucleosynthesis : Element building that occurred in the early universe when the nuclei of primordial matter collided and fused with one another. Most of the helium in the universe was created by this process.

Print Engine : The part of a page printer that does the actual printing (as opposed to making up the image).

Printed Circuit Board (PCB) : A plastics sheet that carries printed metal wiring and sockets for chips and other circuit elements, a module in a hardware unit's overall design.

Printer : Looking rather like typewriters without keyboards or photocopiers, and designed to produce computer output on paper. Dot matrix and daisy wheel printers print one character at a time; line printers print a complete line as one unit; page printers work much like photocopies.

Printout : Output from a computer printer – same as hard copy.

Private Branch Exchange (p(a)bx) : A firm's own telephone exchange (switching centre), installed on its own premises and run by its own staff for the benefit of the users of its extensions.

Probes : Unmanned spacecraft which are launched into space in order to collect data about the solar system and beyond. Space probes are not necessarily designed to return to Earth.

Process Camera : A special camera used to prepare printing plates, especially for offset litho.

Process Control : The automation of a process involves feedback from the system's output to its input and a programme that carries out the tasks involved.

Processor : The part of a computer that actually does the arithmetic and makes the decisions, sometimes called the central processing unit (CPU). In a micro, it is often a microprocessor

Programmable : Describes a general purpose device or system (compared to a dedicated one) which can be programmed for any of a range of tasks.

Programme : An ordered list of instructions for a computer to follow to carry out a given task written in a special language (see below).

Programming Language : There are hundreds of such special languages for giving instructions to computers. All programmes written using them have to be translated into machine code before the computer can obey the instructions.

Project Scheduler : An advanced form of critical path analysis software package.

Prolog : A high level programming language devised by artificial intelligence workers, and suited to developing expert systems.

PROM : Programmable read-only memory (ROM): a memory chip that, once loaded with data, can be read but never written to again (compare with EPROM).

Prominence : A term identifying cloud-like features in the solar atmosphere. The features appear as bright structures in the CORONA above the Solar LIMB and as dark filaments when seen projected against the Solar DISK.

An eruption of gas from the chromosphere of a star. Solar prominences are visible as part of the corona during a total solar eclipse. These eruptions occur above the Sun's surface (photosphere), where gases are suspended in a loop, apparently by magnetic forces that arch upward into the solar corona and then return to the surface.

Aneruption of hot gases above the photosphere of the Sun. Prominences are most easily visible close to the limb of the Sun, but some are also visible as bright streamers on the photosphere.

Promontorium : Cape; headland

Prompt : Any sign given by a computer (a symbol on screen or an audible beep) to show that it awaits a response from the user.

Proper Motion : The apparent motion of a star across the sky (not including a star's parallax), arising from the star's velocity through space with respect to the Sun.

The motion that an object has in the plane of the sky. The direction is in the plane perpendicular to the radial line (see radial velocity). Because the stars are so very far away, their proper motions on the sky are small. One needs to observe for a long time (years) to see proper motions in even relatively nearby stars.

Prophylaxis : A dosing regimen of factor intended to keep factor levels high enough to prevent bleeds from occurring.

Proportional Spacing : A way of printing text so that the space taken up by each character depends on its width – compare the spaces used for i and m in minimum.

Protocol : A set of rules about the format of messages that allows them to be exchanged.

Protogalaxy : Matter that is beginning to come together to form a galaxy. It is the precursor of a present-day galaxy and is sometimes called a "baby galaxy."

Proton : Solar activity levels with at least on high energy event (Class X Flares)

A particle of the hadron family which is one of the two particles that make up atomic nuclei. The proton has a postive electrical charge.

A positively charged elementary particle that resides in the nucleus of every atom.

Proton event : By definition, the measurement of at least 10 Protons/sq.cm/sec/steradian at energies greater than 10 mev.

Proton flare : Any FLARE producing significant fluxes of greater-than-10 mev Protons in the vicinity of the earth.

Proton-proton chain : The series of nuclear fusion steps by which the sun converts four hydrogen nuclei into one helium nucleus and thereby generates energy in its core.

Protons : A sub-atomic particle found in the nuclei of an atom. The proton has a positive charge.

Protoplanet : A small body that attracts gas and dust as it orbits a young star. Eventually, it may form a planetary body.

Protostar : A collection of interstellar gas and dust whose gravitational pull is causing it to collapse on itself and form a star.

A forming star, prior to settling down to the main sequence and burning hydrogen in its core.

Pseudocode : A way of writing algorithms in a form rather like that of a generalized programming language.

Pseudocrater : A generally circular crater produced by a phreatic eruption resulting from emplacement of a lava flow over wet ground.

PSS : Packet switching service: a network dedicated to computer communications that gives higher speeds and lower error rates than the PSTN. The charges for use of a PSS often reflect the length of a message rather than its destination. For overseas communication PSS is often far cheaper than mail or telephone.

PSTN : Public switched telephone network.

Ptolemy 87-150 : (aka Claudius Ptolemaeus) Alexandrian astronomer, mathematician, and geographer who based his astronomy on the belief that all heavenly bodies revolve around the Earth.

Public Switched Telephone Network (PSTN) : The ordinary telephone system, which can be used to transmit data as well as speech using a dial-up connection and charged as for an ordinary telephone call.

Publishing : Preparing material (pure text or with pictures) for others to use – on paper, on microform on magnetic or other kind of disc (e.g. optical publishing), or within a viewdata system (electronic publishing).

Pull-Down Menu : Computer displays sometimes show reminders of the various facilities available, perhaps as icons along the top of the screen. The user positions the pointer suitably, and then presses a key or button to 'pull down' the full menu. For instance, the reminder might concern shading, and the menu would show the shading styles that are available.

Pulsar : A neutron star that emits rapid and periodic pulses of radiation.

A rotating magnetized neutron star that produces regular pulses of radiation when observed from a distance. A pulse is produced every time the rotation brings the magnetic pole region of the neutron star into view. In this way the pulsar acts much as a light house does, sweeping a beam of radiation through space.

Pulsar Glitch : A sudden change in the pulsar period due to a sudden shift in the crust of the neutron star (a "starquake").

Pulsar, Millisecond : As the name implies, these are pulsars with periods measured in terms of milliseconds (thousandths of a second). The shortest have a period of about one and two milliseconds. Millisecond pulsar periods are very constant. They don't slow down much implying a weak magnetic field. Most millisecond pulsars are found in binary systems. It is believed that millisecond pulsars are old pulsars that have had their spin rates increased through the accretion of angular momentum-containing matter from the other star in the binary. Mass transfer has spun up these pulsars back to very fast spin rates. The idea that the millisecond pulsars are actually old systems gains support from the presence of millisecond pulsars in globular clusters.

Pulse Code Modulation (PCM) : A method for sending analogue information in digital form in which the system samples the analog signal frequently, and converts the readings into binary numbers.

Pumice : A light vesicular form of volcanic glass with a high silica content; it is usually light in color and will float on water.

Punched Media : Cards or paper tape punched with holes in patterns which represent data that a suitable computer input device can read – rarely used now.

Pyroclastic : Pertaining to clastic (broken and fragmented) rock material formed by volcanic explosion or aerial expulsion from a volcanic vent.

Q

Quantum mechanics : A theory in physics which is based on 2 ideas: (1) light can be emitted or absorbed only in discrete quantities called quanta, whose energy is proportional to their wavelength; and (2) you can never be exactly sure of the position and velocity of a particle, the more accurately you know the one, the less accurately you can know the other.

Quark : A basic building block of protons, neutrons, and other elementary particles.

Quarks : A Compact, Extra-galactic object which emits huge amounts of energy, but looks like a point of light. Black holes are thought to live at the center of quasars. Several thousand quasars are known. Quasar is actually short for quasi-stellar object (QSO).

A distant energy source which gives off vast amounts of radiation, including radio waves and X-rays.

From quasi-stellar object, a star-like (i.e. Unresolved) object that has a very large luminosity and is located at very large distances from us (as indicated by their high cosmological redshifts). Although technically the term quasar refers to objects that are highly luminous in the radio band, the term tends to be used for both radio-loud and radio-quiet objects high-redshift unresolved objects. Quasars are believed to be powered by supermassive black holes in the centers of galaxies in the process of formation early in the history of the universe.

The brightest type of active galactic nucleus, believed to be powered by a supermassive black hole. The word "quasar" is derived from quasi-stellar radio source, because this type of object was first identified as a kind of radio source. Quasars also are called quasi-stellar objects (qsos). Thousands of quasars have been observed, all at extreme distances from our galaxy.

Queen Victoria : A queen of England (1837) who passed a hemophilia gene to her son, who had hemophilia, and two daughters, who were carriers, and thus to the royal families of Russia, Spain, and Germany.

Query Language : A high level language specially designed for interrogating (asking questions of) a database.

Quiescent prominence (filament) : Long, sheet-like prominences nearly vertical To the solar surface.

Quiet : Solar activity levels with less than one chromospheric event per day.

A descriptive word specifically meaning geomagnetic levels such that Ap < 8 (see Ap INDEX).

Quinkey : A hand-held word processor without a screen into which characters coded by patterns of presses of half a dozen keys are typed. Quinkey can also be used as a direct input device with a computer.

❑❑❑

R

R : The alphabetic letter ("variable") used to denote the distance between the sun and the object being discussed, also called the object's heliocentric distance; in most ephemerides of objects such as comets and minor planets, *r* is given in AU. Similarly, the upper-case Greek letter Delta gives the distance between the object and the earth (its geocentric distance).

Radar *(Radio Detection and Ranging)* **:** A method of detecting, locating, or tracking an object by using beamed, reflected, and timed radio waves. RADAR also refers to the electronic equipment that uses radio waves to detect, locate, and track objects.

A device that bounces radio transmissions off of objects and studies the reflections.

Radial Motion : The component of an object's velocity (speed and direction) as measured along an observer's line of sight.

Radial Velocity : The velocity that an object possesses that is directly toward or away from the observer (hence on a radial line toward or away from the observer). The radial velocity can be determined using the doppler shift.

Radian : A unit of angle equal to about 57 degrees. The length along the arc of a circle covering by one radian is equal to the radius of the circle. The complete angle around the circle (360 degrees) is equal to 2 pi radians. The radian is particularly useful because if you know the distance to some object and you measure its apparent size as the angle it subtends in your field of view in radians, then the actual size is just that number of radians times the distance to the object. For example, a meter stick held up at a distance of 100 meters makes an apparent angle in your field of view of 0.01 radians.

Radiant : The point where the backward projection of the meteor trajectory intersects the celestial sphere. More generally, the point in the sky where meteors from a specific shower seem to come from.

Radiation : Energy radiated in the form of waves or particles; photons.

The process by which electromagnetic energy moves through space as vibrations in electric and magnetic fields. This term also refers to radiant energy and other forms of electromagnetic radiation, such as gamma rays and X-rays.

Radiation Belt : Regions of charged particles in a magnetosphere.

Radiative Energy Transport : While photons carry energy at the velocity of light, they are unable to travel very far in the interiors of stars before they are absorbed. When re-emitted, the energy may well be emitted in a totally different direction from that in which the original photon was moving. Photons thus follow a "random walk" as they pass through an absorbing region and typically can take a million years to carry energy from the centre of the Sun to the surface. Nonetheless, photons will be the mechanism of choice in a star except in those places and at those times when they are unable to maintain equilibrium. In such regions, convection will occur.

Radiative Process : An event involving the emission or absorption of radiation. For example, a hydrogen atom that absorbs a photon of light converts the energy of that radiation into electrical potential energy.

Radiative Transport : The direct transport of energy via light (electromagnetic radiation). How fast radiation can carry heat through a star is determined by the opacity of the star. When you feel heat coming off a fire you are getting that heat through direct (infrared) radiation from the fire—an example of radiative transport.

Radio emission : Emissions of the sun in radio wavelengths from centimeters To dekameters, under both quiet and disturbed conditions. Type I. A noise storm composed of many short, narrow-band bursts In the metric range (300 - 50 mhz). Type II. Narrow-band emission that begins in the meter range (300 mhz) and sweeps slowly (tens of minutes) toward deka-Meter wavelengths (10 mhz). Type II emissions occur in Loose association with major flares and are indicative of A shock wave moving through the solar atmosphere. Type III. Narrow-band bursts that sweep rapidly (seconds) from Decimeter to dekameter wavelengths (500 - 0.5 mhz). They Often occur in groups and are an occasional feature of complex Solar ACTIVE regions. Type IV. A smooth continuum of broad-band bursts primarily in the Meter range (300 - 30 mhz). These bursts are associated with Some major flare events beginning 10 to 20 minutes after the Flare maximum, and can last for hours.

Radio event : Flares with Centimetric Bursts and/or definite Ionospheric Event (SID).

Radio Galaxy : A galaxy that is emitting most of its energy in the form of radio waves rather than light in or near the visible bands where stars emit most of their radiation. This means that radio galaxies are dominated by some non-stellar process.

Radio observations : Two main methods are used, forward scatter observations and radar observations. The first are easy to carry out, but deliver only data on the general meteor activity; showers cannot be associated. The last is carried out by professional astronomers. Meteor radiants and meteoroid orbits can be determined.

Radio Telescope : A telescope that receives radio emissions from celestial bodies. The key difference between radars and radio telescopes is that radars actively probe an object by emitted radio waves and a radio telescope passively receives radio waves.

A type of electromagnetic radiation which has the lowest frequency, the longest wavelength, and is produced by charged particles moving back and forth. Radio waves are not blocked by clouds in the Earth's atmosphere.

Radiation with the longest wavelengths and smallest frequencies and energies in the electromagnetic spectrum.

Radioactivity : The spontaneous decay of certain rare, unstable, atomic nuclei into more stable atomic nuclei. A natural by-product of this process is the release of energy.

Radius : The radius of a star or planet is the distance from the center of the star or planet out to its surface. Radius is equal to half the diameter. Star sizes are often compared to the solar radius which is 7×10^{10} cm.

RAM : A form of memory used in computers, the data in which can be changed as well as accessed.

Random Access : Direct access.

Raster : Pattern of lines on a television screen.

Reaction Wheel : One of four spinning flywheels aboard the Hubble Space Telescope. The flywheels work together to make the observatory rotate either more rapidly or less rapidly toward a new target.

Read : A drive reads information from a disc when it retrieves a copy of it (and writes when it records data on to it).

Read and Write Memory (RAM) : The storage space inside a computer where data is stored while it is in use. Its contents are constantly being overwritten as different programmes run, and may be lost altogether when the computer is switched off.

Read Only : Describes anything that can be read from but not written to, such as a protected disc or ROM.

Read-Only Memory (ROM) : Part of a computer's internal memory that stores software in frequent use. Unlike RAM, the contents of ROM are not lost when you switch off (see also *EPROM*).

Real Time : Describes a system that reacts to each input as soon as it receives it, e.g. in interactive use or when controlling events as they happen. A real-time clock in a computer system keeps a tally of day, date and time for use or display when needed.

Recessional Velocity : The velocity at which an object moves away from an observer. The recessional velocity of a distant galaxy is proportional to its distance from Earth. Therefore, the greater the recessional velocity, the more distant the object.

Record : Each file in a database consists of a number of records, each of which contain various fields for storing units of information. For instance, a firm's customer file might contain details of thousands of companies, with a separate record for each one. To record information on a disc or tape is to store it for future access.

Recovery Phase : Of a geomagnetic storm, that period when the

Recurrence : Used especially in reference to the recurrence of physical Parameters every 27 days (the rotation period of the sun).

Red giant : A star that has low surface temperature and a diameter that is large relative to the Sun.

A star with low surface temperature (thus red) and large size (giant). These stars are found on the upper-right hand side of the HR diagram. The red giant phase in a star's life occurs after it has left the main sequence. The Sun will become a red giant in about 5 billion years.

Red Giant Star : An old, bright star, much larger and cooler than the Sun. Betelgeuse (alpha Orionis) is an example of a red giant.

Redshift : The lengthening of a light wave from an object that is moving away from an observer. For example, when a galaxy is traveling away from Earth, its light shifts to the red end of the electromagnetic spectrum.

A redshift caused by the expansion of space. The wavelength of light increases as it traverses the expanding universe between its point of emission and its point of detection by the same amount that space has expanded during the crossing time.

Redundancy : The extent to which parts of a message can be predicted from a knowledge of the other parts. A large proportion of a highly redundant message can be destroyed without loss of meaning. In general, redundancy means duplication.

Reflection Nebula : A nebula composed of dust particles that scatter and reflect incident light (rather than glowing from their own intrinsic emission). Dust preferentially scatters short wavelengths, so reflection nebulae have a characteristic blue appearance.

Often (in the Pleiades, for example) we find hot, young stars still closely associated with the dusty material out of which they formed. In such situations, the remaining dust reflects the light of the stars (as evidenced by its blue colour and the fact that the spectrum of the light is the same as that of the stars).

Reflective : Depends on light being reflected (bounced) from a surface.

Reflector : A telescope that uses as its primary optical element a mirror. Nearly all large telescopes in use today by amateur and professional astronomers are reflecting telescopes.

A type of telescope, also known as a reflecting telescope, that uses one or more polished, curved mirrors to gather light and reflect it to a focal point.

Refractor : A telescope that uses as its primary optical element a lens. Binoculars are a type of refractor. In general, refractors are much more expensive to build and buy than are reflectors.

A telescope, also known as a refracting telescope, that uses a transparent lens to gather light and bend it to a focus.

Refresh Rate : The frequency with which a system renews the content of a screen or memory. If the rate is too low in the former case, a flicker may result.

Regenerator : A device that detects, boosts and retransmits an input digital signal (compare with repeater). Because digital signals suffer from interference less than analog ones, regenerators can be further apart than repeaters.

Regio :Region.

Regolith : The layer of loose rock resting on bedrock (sometimes called mantle rock), found on the Earth, the Moon, or a planet. Regolith is made up of soils, sediments, weathered rock, and hard, near-surface crusts. On the surface of the Moon, regolith is a fine rocky layer of fragmentary debris (or dust) produced mainly by meteoroid collisions.

The layer of rocky debris and dust made by metoritic impact that forms the uppermost surface of planets, satellites and asteroids.

Regular Galaxy Cluster : These are great groupings of galaxies into huge spherical distributions that have large numbers of galaxies concentrated in their centers. The tend to contain thousands of galaxies and to have many bright elliptical and S0 type galaxies.

Relational : Describes a database management system that represents some of the complicated relationships that exist in the real world between the items of information that it stores.

Relativity : A theory of physics that describes the dynamical behavior of matter and energy. The consequences of relativity can be quite strange at very high velocities and very high densities. A direct result of the theory of relativity is the equation $E = mc^2$, which expresses a relationship between mass (m), energy (E), and the speed of light (c).

Theory of More accurately describes the motions of bodies in strong gravitational fields or near the speed of light than newtonian mechanics. All experiments done to date agree with relativity's predictions to a high degree of accuracy. (Curiously, Einstein received the Nobel prize in 1921 not specifically for Relativity but rather for his 1905 work on the photoelectric effect and "services to Theoretical Physics".)

Relativity, General : Einstein's theory of relativity incorporating the force of gravity into the special theory of relativity. This theory incorporates gravity into the nature of space and time. It predicts, among other things, the existence of gravitational radiation and black holes.

Relativity, Special : The specific set of rules relating observations in one inertial frame of reference to the observations of the same phenomenon in another inertial frame of reference. Einstein's theory of special relativity ensures that the laws of physics for mechanicsl and for electromagnetism are the same for all such observers. It postulates that the speed of light is the same for all observers. One of its more famous consequences is the equivalence of matter and energy through the equation $E = mc^2$.

Relaxation : Freedom from anxiety and tension, both physiologically and psychologically. Relaxation techniques are aimed at reducing anxiety and diverting attention away from pain by voluntary relaxation of the muscles of the body.

Relay : As a verb, to pass on information; as a noun, an electromagnetic switch.

Remote : Not permanently online, non-local.

Repeater : A device, placed in a long cable, that strengthens passing signals. Without repeaters, the signals would be too weak to detect at the end. Repeaters work on analog principles, and tend to amplify noise as well as signals (contrast regenerator).

Replacement Therapy : In hemophilia, the infusion of clotting factor(s) to serve as a temporary substitute for the body's missing or deficient factor. In hemophilia A, factor VIII is infused as the replacement therapy.

Report : A user-defined summary of, or extract from, information held in a database, a report generator being a programme that can extract, sort and collate information for this purpose.

Resident : Permanently fitted in a computer, e.g. held in ROM.

Resistance : The way a wire will oppose the passage of an electric current, thus reducing its size.

Resolution : A measure of the quality of printout and of computer displays and graphics, for instance. The higher the resolution, the finer the detail (see also pixel).

The amount of small detail visible in an image; low resolution shows only large features, high resolution shows many small details

Resonance : A relationship in which the orbital period of one body is related to that of another by a simple integer fraction, such as 1/2, 2/3, 3/5.

A state in which one orbiting object is subject to periodic gravitational perturbations by another.

Reticulum : Reticular (net-like) pattern

Retrograde : Having a direction which is opposite that of similar bodies.

Rotation or orbital motion in a clockwise direction when viewed from above the north pole of the primary (i.e. In the opposite sense to most satellites); the opposite of direct. The north pole is the one on the same side of the ecliptic as the Earth's north pole.

The rotation or orbital motion of an object in a clockwise direction when viewed from the north pole of the ecliptic; moving in the opposite sense from the great majority of solar system bodies.

Revolution : The circling of a smaller object around a larger object.

The orbital motion of one object around another. The Earth revolves around the Sun in one year. The moon revolves around the Earth in approximately 28 days.

RF : Radio frequency: electromagnetic waves of frequency suitable for radio transmission (roughly in the 10 kHz to 10 MHz range).

RGB : Red-green-blue: describes a colour monitor which handles the three primary video colour signals separately. It gives excellent displays of colour computer graphics compared with a colour TV set.

Rhyolite : Fine-grained extrusive igneous rock, commonly with phenocrysts of quartz and feldspar in a glassy groundmass.

Rift : A fracture or crack in a planet's surface caused by extension. On some volcanoes, subsurface intrusions are concentrated in certain directions; this causes tension at the surface and also means that there will be more eruptions in these "rift zones."

Rift valley : An elongated valley formed by the depression of a block of the planet's crust between two faults or groups of faults of approximately parallel strike.

Right Ascension (R.A.) : A coordinate used on the celestial sphere just as longitude is used on Earth. An object's right ascension is measured in hours and minutes eastward from the vernal equinox.

A coordinate used by astronomers to locate stars and other celestial objects in the sky. Right ascension is comparable to longitude, but it is measured in hours, minutes, and seconds because the entire sky appears to pass overhead over a period of 24 hours. The zero hour corresponds to the apparent location of the Sun with respect to the stars on the day of the vernal (spring) equinox (approximately March 21).

The angular distance of an object measured eastwards along the celestial equator.

One element of the astronomical coordinate system on the sky, which can be though of as longitude on the earth projected onto the sky. Right ascension is usually denoted by the lower-case Greek letter alpha and is measured eastward in hours, minutes, and seconds of time from the vernal equinox. There are 24 hours of right ascension, though the 24-hour line is always taken as 0 hours. More rarely, one sometimes sees right ascension in degrees, in which case there are 360 degrees of right ascension to make a complete circuit of the sky. When specifying a comet's location on the sky, one must state the right ascension and declination (with equinox), along with date and time (since a comet moves with respect to the background stars). For examples of how right ascension (R.A.) and declination (Decl.) Appear on a star atlas, see the Millennium Atlas (also here and here). Note that, at the celestial equator, there are 15 arc seconds in one second of R.A. (often stated as "one second of time"); as one moves away from the celestial equator, one must multiply this factor of 15 by an additional factor (cosine of the declination), because the lines of right ascension get closer and closer as one nears the celestial poles, to get straight-line distances between two celestial objects that are close to each other (for long distances across the celestial sphere, a more complex formula is used). Thus, when the R.A. is given in h, m, and s, it is usually given in seconds of time to one more significant digit than is the Decl. In arcsec (i.e., if R.A. is given to 0s.01, the Decl. Should be only given to 0".1, though this significant-figures requirement disappears as one approaches the celestial poles).

Rigid Disc : Another name for hard disc (as opposed to floppy).

Rima : A fissure.

Ring : A network design where all the devices form a closed loop. Data goes the same way round the ring all the time, with only the device addressed taking a copy of a given chunk; the source device removes the data when it gets back to it.

Riometer (Relative Ionospheric Opacity meter) **:** A specially designed radio Receiver for continuous monitoring of cosmic noise. The Absorption of cosmic noise in the polar regions is very Sensitive to the solar low-energy cosmic ray flux.

Robot : A machine that can be programmed to drive motors to do a variety of jobs automatically, often being controlled by a microprocessor.

Robotic Optical Transient Search Experiment (ROTSE) **:** A terrestrial telescope that searches for the optical counterparts of gamma-ray bursts. When orbiting satellites detect a gamma-ray burst, ROTSE begins searching for its visible-light afterglow. ROTSE-I (an array of four electronic telephoto cameras) and ROTSE-II (a set of identical telescopes) are located in Los Alamos, New Mexico.

Robust : Describes environment-proof hardware, software that is unlikely to crash (fail), or signals unlikely to be corrupted.

Roche limit : The closest a fluid body can orbit to its primary without being pulled apart by tidal forces. A solid body may survive within the Roche limit if the tidal forces do not exceed its structural strength. The Roche limit is calculated with the equation RL = 2.456*R*(p'/p)^(1/3)

The Roche Limit was first described by Edouard Roche in 1848. It is the closest distance a body can come to a planet without being pulled apart by the planet's tidal (gravity) force. As a result, large moons cannot survive inside the Roche Limit. On July 7, 1992, Comet Shoemaker-Levy 9 broke apart into 21 pieces due to tidal forces when it passed within Jupiter's Roche Limit; on the subsequent pass, each of the comet's pieces collided with Jupiter. If a planet and a moon have identical densities, then the Roche Limit is 2.446 times the radius of the planet. The Roche Limits for the ringed planets are: Jupiter - 175,000 km (108,000 miles) Saturn - 147,000 km (92,000 miles) Uranus - 62,000 km (39,000 miles) Neptune - 59,000 km (37,000 miles) This limit represents the rough boundary between each planet's ring system and its innermost moons.

The smallest distance at which two celestial bodies can remain in a stable orbit around each other without one of them being torn apart by tidal forces. The distance depends on the densities of the two bodies and their orbit around each other.

Roche Lobe : The region surrounding a star in a binary system inside of which the star's material is gravitationally bound to the star. If a star exceeds its Roche lobe it can become a semidetached binary. Two binary stars that share a Roche lobe constitute a contact binary.

Role Playing : Acting out the thoughts, feelings, and behaviors of another person or role, such as a doctor.

ROM : Read-only memory.

Rotation : The spin of an object around its central axis. Earth rotates about its axis every 24 hours. A spinning top rotates about its center shaft. The spin of a planet on its axis.

Rotation Curve : A plot of the orbital velocity in the disk of a galaxy versus the radius from the center of the galaxy. This curve can then be used to obtain the mass within a given radius (by using Kepler's laws for orbital dynamics). Typically rotation curves suggest that galaxies have considerably more matter than that associated with the visible stars (see dark matter).

R-Process : The huge numbers of neutrons given off during a supernova explosion allow for the rapid (hence "r") absorption of neutrons by various elements which transforms them into elements higher up in the periodic table. This is an important step in the process of nucleosynthesis.

RR Lyrae Variables : A variable star that has a regularly varying luminosity. These stars all have about the same luminosity making them suitable for obtaining distances. They are not as useful as Cepheid variables, however, because they are not as luminous.

RS232 : A standard, developed for telecommunications equipment, that concerns serial information transfer at one of a standard range of speeds. The standard has been adopted widely by computer manufacturers, so that many computers have an RS232 or similar port for connecting them to peripherals.

Rupes : The term applied to scarps on planetary surfaces; many scarps are thought to be the surface expression of faults within the crust of the planetary object. Scarp.

Russell-Vogt theorem : "The equilibrium structure of a normal star is uniquely dependent on its mass and chemical composition." This principle allows us with confidence to approach the structure of individual stars knowing only their mass and composition.

❑❑❑

S

Sapping : A process of erosion where water leaks to the surface through the pores of rocks; as the water flows away, it slowly removes material to form valleys and channel networks.

Satellite : A body that revolves around a larger body.

An object that revolves around a larger primary body. Satellites may be naturally occurring, such as the Moon, or they may be man-made, such as the *Hubble Space Telescope* and the *Compton Gamma-Ray Observatory*.

A major use of artificial earth satellites is for the transfer of signals, although monitoring (traffic or weather, for instance) is also relevant. Modern communications satellites are active: they pick up and boost radio and TV signals before re- transmitting them, rather than acting as simple reflectors (see also direct broadcast (by) satellite and geostationary satellite).

Satellite TV : The relay of TV signals by communications satellites.

Saturn : Saturn has an orbit of almost 1.5 billion km. It is the second biggest planet and is a gas giant planet. Check out SEDS' Nine Planets, for more about planets.

The sixth planet in the solar system, noted for its obvious ring structure. Saturn is almost ten times the Earth's distance from the Sun. The planet completes a circuit around the Sun in about 30 Earth years. Saturn is the second largest and the least dense planet in our solar system. The planet has more than 21 moons, including Titan, the second largest known moon in our solar system.

Save : To copy data from a computer's main memory to backing store (usually in magnetic form, e.g. on to a disc).

Scan : To pass across a page cell by cell, and down row by row, perhaps to produce a digital version. A scanner is a digitizer used in this way.

Scarp : Line of cliffs produced by faulting or erosion.

A line of cliffs produced by faulting or erosion; a relatively straight, clifflike face or slope of considerable linear extent, breaking the general continuity of the land by separating surfaces lying at different levels.

Schiaparelli, Giovanni Virginio 1835-1910 : Italian astronomer who in 1877 first observed the "canals" on Mars. He believed that the features he observed included straight lines that joined in a complicated pattern. He called these lines 'canali', which means 'channels'. However, the Italian word was mistranslated into the English word 'canals'. That, combined with the suspicious straightness of the lines, bespoke of artificial structures, and this created a furor. Speculations concerning the possibility of intelligent life on Mars sprang up in the popular press. Even astronomers felt the pull of that dramatic possibility. Foremost among these was Percival Lowell, who carried matters far beyond Schiaparelli.

Schwarzchild Radius : The distance from the "center" of a black hole to its "edge" (called an event horizon). If the Earth became a black hole, all of its mass would be squeezed into a sphere with a Schwarzschild radius of 0.03 cm, about the size of a bacterium.

The radius of the event horizon surrounding a nonrotating black hole. Its size is given by $R_s = 2GM / c^2$. For a one solar mass star this is about 3 kilometers.

A lobate or irregular scarp.

Scout : A message sent through a network to check whether a terminal at the far end is ready to receive data or not.

Scramble : To disguise a message (for instance) so that only authorized people can access it.

Screen : Output device, such as a monitor, TV set or flat LCD; a method of shading printed text and the effect produced.

Screen Dump : The contents of a screen (text and/or graphics) printed as a whole on to paper.

Scroll : When output material is larger than a screen, the processor makes the text seem to move up so that the display can show it 'page' by 'page'. Most systems scroll up and down when required; some (such as spreadsheets) also need to be able to scroll from side to side.

SCVF : Single channel voice frequency.

Search : To hunt through a file or database for specified types of information.

SECAM : Sequential couleur â mémoire: a colour TV standard developed in France and adopted by Eastern European countries and parts of the Middle East and North Africa.

Secondary Atmosphere : A gas or gases, such as helium, that a planet discharges from its interior after having lost its primary or primordial atmosphere.

Secondary Mirror : A small mirror in a reflecting telescope that redirects light from the larger primary mirror toward the light-sensitive scientific instruments. In a Cassegrain-type telescope like the Hubble Space Telescope, the secondary mirror is slightly convex and directs light from the primary mirror back through a hole in the center of the primary mirror. Hubble's secondary mirror measures 12.2 inches (0.3 meters) in diameter.

Sector boundary : In the SOLAR WIND, the area of demarcation between sec-Tors, which are large-scale features distinguished by the Predominant direction of the interplanetary magnetic field, Toward or away from the sun.

Secular motion : Secular variations in the motions of the planets are those that have very slow changes that proceed through ages (*secula*) in a way such that they are nearly proportional with time for a relatively large number of years. Precession is considered a secular variation, arising from the motions of the mean equator and the mean ecliptic. Compare this with periodic variations, which are rather rapid changes; nutation is a periodic variation.

Seismic Wave : The transfer of energy throughout a celestial object, such as a planet, resulting from an external impact or an internal event. On Earth, seismic waves are generated primarily by earthquakes.

Selection effects : Astronomy relies heavily on statistical inference in drawing its conclusions. Statistical samples must be unbiased. For example, there is a famous example in astronomy where the size and structure deduced for the "universe" was completely wrong because the impact of interstellar dust was unknown. This bias, or selection effect, led to invalid conclusions. A more routine example might be surveys based on biased selections (heights of U of T students taken in the men's gym before a basketball game, for example).

Self-Expression : Expression of who you are and how you feel through a wide variety of activities—art, play, music, dramatic play, quiet time, and communicating with others.

Semi-Conductor : A substance like silicon, whose poor electrical conductivity is very easy to vary in order to build up complex circuit elements.

Semidetached Binary : A binary system where one star is too large and some of its outer layer transfers over to and falls onto its binary companion star. Semidetached binary stars can form accretion disks.

Semi-major Axis : The length of the semi-major axis of an orbit ellipse. For solar system bodies, the value of semi-major axis is typically denoted by *a* and expressed in units of AU.

Abbr. A, half the length of the major axis of an ellipse, a standard element used to describe an elliptical orbit.

The semimajor axis of an ellipse (e.g. A planetary orbit) is 1/2 the length of the major axis which is a segment of a line passing thru the foci of the ellipse with endpoints on the ellipse itself. The semimajor axis of a planetary orbit is also the average distance from the planet to its primary. The periapsis and apoapsis distances can be calculated from the semimajor axis and the eccentricity by rp = a(1-e) and ra = a(1+e).

Sensor : A device that detects touch, temperature, sound, acidity or some other similar (analog) physical or chemical information, with a corresponding electrical output, thus able to allow computers and robots to react to their environment.

Sensory Experiences : Experiences that stimulate the sensory system and allow children to receive and interpret information about their environment.

Serial Access : When something must be searched through from the beginning (as with a cassette tape) instead of being able to jump to any part of it directly (as with a floppy or compact disc)

Serial Interface : Connection between two devices that transfers information only one bit at a time (compare with parallel interface).

Server : A hardware and software unit with the function of looking after the needs of a single peripheral – thus a file server works with a drive.

Severe Geomagnetic Storm : A storm for which the Ap index was100 or more.

Seyfert Galaxy : A galaxy characterized by a moderately bright, compact active galactic nucleus, presumably powered by a black hole.

Seyferts are spirals galaxies that have bright starlike cores. Seyferts have strong emission lines, and the emission lines are very broad, implying velocities from 500 to 4000 km/sec. Seyferts are classified into two types based on the width of their emission lines. Seyferts with very broad Hydrogen emission lines are called Type I, and Seyferts with more narrow Hydrogen emission lines are called Type II. Many Seyferts also have compact radio sources at their centers.

Shakespeare, William 1564-1616 : English playwright and poet; wrote some good skits.

Shared Logic : When a number of terminals share the same processor, the system may be called shared logic (or shared processing). Now that processor power has become so cheap, networked micros are often preferable instead.

Shared Processing : See shared logic.

Shatter Cone : Striated conical fracture surfaces produced by meteorite impact into fine-grained, brittle rocks such as limestone.

Shell Burning : In later stages of a stars life regions of the envelope become hot enough to begin nuclear burning. These burning regions lie in a shell surrounding the core. For example, helium burning might take place in the core (where the hydrogen has been exhausted) with a shell of hydrogen burning surrounding it. There can be more than one region of shell burning, each shell with its own nuclear reactions.

Shell Source : As the nuclear fuel in the core of a star becomes exhausted, the fusion process may well continue in a shell surrounding the core. In fact, for stars undergoing successive stages of nuclear burning, we can find a number of shells burning, H at the furthest from the core, He closer in, and so on.

Shepherd Satellite : (or 'shepherd moon') a satellite which constrains the extent of a planetary ring through gravitational forces.

Shield : Any of several extensive regions where ancient Precambrian crystalline rocks are exposed at the Earth's surface.

Shield Volcano : A volcano in the shape of a flattened dome, broad and low, built by flows of very fluid lava.

Shock Metamorphism : The production of irreversible chemical or physical changes in rocks by a shock wave generated by impact, or detonation of high-explosive or nuclear devices.

Shock Wave : A high-pressure wave that travels at supersonic speeds. Shock waves are usually produced by an explosion.

Short Wave ; Describes radio signals with short wavelengths and high frequencies.

Short wave fade (SWF) : A particular ionospheric solar flare effect under The broad category of sudden ionospheric disturbances (sids) Whereby short-wavelength radio transmissions, VLF, through HF, are absorbed for a period of minutes to hours.

Short-Period Comet : Comets that orbit mainly in the inner solar system. Usually these objects orbit the Sun in less than 200 years. Halley's comet is an example of a short-period comet.

Shredder : Machine that shreds paper (for instance, computer printout) after use so that it cannot be read.

Sidereal : Of, relating to, or concerned with the stars. Sidereal rotation is that measured with respect to the stars rather than with respect to the Sun or the primary of a satellite.

Sidereal Day : The period of rotation of an object with respect to the stars. Compare this to a solar day, which is the period of rotation of an object with respect to the Sun. On Earth a sidereal day is 23 hours, 56 minutes and 4 seconds, while the solar day is 24 hours.

Sidereal month : The average period of revolution of the moon around the earth in reference to a fixed star, equal to 27 days, 7 hours, 43 minutes in units of mean solar time.

Siderial rotation : Rotation time measured with respect to the fixed stars rather than the Sun or body orbited.

Siderophile elements : This phrase literally means *iron-loving* elements. It includes Iridium, Osmium, Platinum and Plladium, which are found in the metal-rich interiors of chemically segregated asteroids and planets; consequently, these elements are extremely rare on Earth's surface.

Signal : Any energy transfer that carries information from place to place, such as a radio broadcast, speech in a telephone system, or computer data on its way to a peripheral.

Signal to Noise Ratio : A signal always picks up noise which affects reception. The higher the signal to noise ratio, the clearer the signal will be at the receiving end.

Silicate : A rock or mineral whose structure is dominated by bonds of silicon and oxygen atoms. A compound containing silicon and oxygen (e.g. Olivine)

Silicon : A non-metallic chemical element.

Simplex : Describes a communication channel in which messages can be sent in only one direction (contrast half-duplex and duplex).

Simulator : Device or software system that accurately represents something that is too large, expensive, dangerous or difficult to practise on direct; used for training and sometimes also for research.

Single Channel Voice Frequency (SCVF) : British Telecom's new-style telex system.

Singularity : 1. A black hole's center, where the matter is thought to be infinitely dense, the volume is infinitely small, and the force of gravity is infinitely large. 2. In classical general relativity, a location at which physical quantities such as density become infinite. A singularity lies at the center of a black hole.

Sinus : Literally "bay"; really a small plain

Skew : Data skew.

Slow-Scan TV : Involves TV pictures shot at one frame every few seconds instead of 25 or 30 a second. The effect is like a rapid succession of still photographs, but the output takes far less bandwidth to transmit than normal TV signals. Slow-scan TV is useful for security purposes, and in situations where the cost of transmitting true moving pictures is not justified, such as a business video-conference.

Smart Card : A type of credit card, for instance, which carries a chip to provide processing power and memory.

Smart Device : Intelligent device (as opposed to being dumb).

Smoothed sunspot number : An average of 13 monthly RI numbers, centered on The month of concern.

Software : Includes programmes and associated data. A software generator is a programme that reduces the labour of routine programming. A software tool is any utility that helps to make programming faster and easier.

Solar prominences : Gases trapped at the edge of the Sun which appear to shoot outward from the Sun's surface.

Solar system : The Sun and all of the planets, comets, etc. Which revolve around it.

Solar Arrays : Two rigid, wing-like arrays of solar panels that convert sunlight directly into electricity to operate the Hubble Space Telescope's scientific instruments, computers, and radio transmitters. Some of the energy generated is stored in onboard batteries so the telescope can operate while in Earth's shadow (which is about 36 minutes out of each 97-minute orbit). The solar arrays are designed for replacement by visiting astronauts during servicing missions.

Solar Constant : The average amount of solar radiation reaching a planet; usually expressed in watts (energy per unit time) per square meter. For Earth, the solar constant equals 1,372 W/m^2. Each planet has a unique solar constant depending on its distance from the Sun.

Solar coordinates : Central Meridian Distance (CMD). The angular distance in solar Longitude measured from the central meridian.

Solar cycle : The approximately 11-year quasi-periodic variation in frequency or number of solar active events.

The periodic changing of the Sun's magnetic field, which determines the number of sunspots and the amount of particles emitted in the solar wind. The period of the cycle is about 11 years.

Solar Eclipse : A phenomenon in which the Moon's disk passes in front of the Sun, blocking sunlight. A total eclipse occurs when the Moon completely obscures the Sun's disk, leaving only the solar corona visible. A solar eclipse can only occur during a new phase of the Moon.

A shadow which falls on an area of Earth when the Moon moves between the Sun and Earth.

Solar flares : A magnetic storm on the Sun's surface which shows up as a sudden increase in brightness.

Solar longitude : Angular distance along the Earth's orbit measured from the intersection of the ecliptic and the celestial equator where the Sun moves from south to north. It gives the position of the Earth on its orbit and, hence, is a more appropriate information on a meteor shower's maximum than the date.

Solar maximum : The month(s) during the SOLAR CYCLE when the 12-month mean Of monthly average SUNSPOT NUMBERS reaches a maximum. The most Recent solar maximum occurred in July 1989.

Solar Maximum : The midpoint in the solar cycle where the amount of sunspot activity and the output of cosmic particles and solar radiation is highest.

The beginning and the end of a sunspot cycle when only a few sunspots are usually observed, and the output of particles and radiation is normal.

The month(s) during the SOLAR CYCLE when the 12-month mean Of monthly average SUNSPOT NUMBERS reaches a minimum. The most recent minimum occurred in September 1986.

Solar nebula : The large cloud of gas and dust from which the Sun and planets condensed 4.6 billion years ago.

Solar sector boundary (SSB) : The apparent solar origin, or base, of the Interplanetary SECTOR BOUNDARY marked by the larger-scale polarity Inversion lines.

Solar System : Any system composed of one or more stars and one or more planets or other celestial bodies gravitationally bound to the star(s). Although most solar systems are binaries (meaning that they have two stars), our own solar system is composed of one star (named Sol, but commonly called the Sun), nine planets, and other, smaller stuff. Since 99% of the mass in the solar system is in the Sun and Jupiter, astrophysicists like to joke that our solar system is composed of the Sun, Jupiter, and other stuff. This probably says more about astrophysicists than it does about our solar system. The Sun and its surrounding matter, including asteroids, comets, planets and moons, held together by the Sun's gravitational influence.

Solar wind : The outward flux of solar particles and magnetic fields from the.

A continuous stream of charged particles which are released from the Sun and hurled outward into space at speeds up to 800 kilometers per second. Solar winds are very prominent after solar flare activity.

A tenuous flow of gas and energetic charged particles, mostly protons and electrons — plasma -- which stream from the Sun; typical solar wind velocities are near 350 kilometers per second. (217 miles) per second.

Streams of charged particles flowing from the Sun at millions of kilometers per hour. This high-speed solar wind varies in composition, always streams away from the Sun, and interacts with other regions of matter in the solar system.

The flow of energetic charged particles from the sun's corona.

Solar wings : A panel of solar cells which converts sunlight into electrical energy.

Solstice : The position of the Sun when it reaches its northernmost declination (summer) or southernmost declination (winter).

Sort : To re-order the contents of a data file on the basis of the user's needs at the time.

Source Programme : Instructions written in a programming language before they have been translated by a compiler into an object programme for a processor to obey.

South Celestial Pole (SCP) : A direction determined by the projection of the Earth's South Pole onto the celestial sphere. The SCP is exactly 180 degrees from the North Celestial Pole and corresponds to a declination of –90 degrees.

Space Infrared Telescope Facility (SIRTF) : A space-borne infrared telescope that will study planets, comets, stars, galaxies, and other celestial objects. NASA plans to launch SIRTF in December 2002 on a Delta rocket. SIRTF represents the fourth and final satellite in NASA's Great Observatories program, which includes the Hubble Space Telescope and the Chandra X-Ray Observatory.

Space Shuttle : A reusable U.S. spacecraft operated by astronauts and used to transport cargo, such as satellites, into space. The spacecraft uses rockets to launch into space, but it lands like an airplane. A space shuttle carried the Hubble Space Telescope into space in 1990. Astronauts aboard subsequent space shuttles have visited the telescope to service it.

Space Telescope Imaging Spectrograph (STIS) : An instrument that acts like a prism to separate light from the cosmos into its component colors, providing a wavelength "fingerprint" of the object being observed. The information yields clues about an object's temperature, chemical composition, density, and motion. Spectrographic observations also reveal changes in celestial objects as the universe evolves. Astronauts installed STIS aboard the Hubble Space Telescope in February 1997 during the Second Servicing Mission. STIS spans ultraviolet, visible, and near-infrared wavelengths. The spectrograph can sample 500 points along a celestial object simultaneously.

Space Telescope Science Institute (stsci) : The astronomical research center responsible for operating the Hubble Space Telescope as an international scientific observatory. Located in Baltimore, Maryland, stsci is managed by AURA (Association of Universities for Research in Astronomy) under contract to the National Aeronautics and Space Administration (NASA) and the National Science Foundation (NSF).

Spacetime : The four-dimensional coordinate system (three dimensions of space and one of time) in which physical events are located.

Spatial Awareness :An understanding of the area and objects in proximity to oneself.

Spatter cone : A low, steep-sided cone built up from fluid pyroclasts coating the surface around a vent.

SPC : Stored programme control.

Speaker : A device with an electrical input and a corresponding sound output.

Special Effects Unit : A system able to produce special video effects in programme making, such as shaping a sequence over the surface of a sphere or mixing shots by apparently turning pages.

Spectral Class (Spectral Type) : A classification scheme that groups stars according to their surface temperatures and spectral features.

Spectral Line : In a spectrum, an emission (bright) or absorption (dark) at a specific frequency or wavelength.

Spectral Type : A system of classification for stars based on the presence and strength of various types of emission lines in their spectrum. Basically the spectral type is a measure of the surface temperature of the star since the temperature determines which emission lines will be present and how strong they will be. From hottest to coolest stars are grouped into categories O, B, A, F, G, K, and M. Each letter is subdivided into 10 numbers, from hotter to cooler 0, 1, 2, 3, 4, etc.

Spectrograph (Spectrometer) **:** An instrument that spreads electromagnetic radiation into its component frequencies and wavelengths for detailed study. A spectrograph is similar to a prism, which spreads white light into a continuous rainbow.

Spectrograph : The image of the electromagnetic spectrum produced by a spectroscope.

Spectroradiometer [SPEC-tro-RAY-dee-om-it-er] : A device that measures the amount of reflected or radiated energy from a surface in two or more wavelengths.

SPECTROSCOPE : An instrument which separates visible light into its various wavelengths. Each wavelength corresponds to a specific color in the spectrum.

Spectroscopic Binary : Binary stars whose binary nature is determined by observations of their spectra. Periodic doppler shifts in emission or absorption lines reveal that the stars are moving in orbits even when the separate stars cannot be resolved in direct observations.

Spectroscopic parallax : As used in class, this term refers to the determination of the absolute magnitude of a star (or the stars in a cluster) in relation to the main sequence stars by noting its spectral class. If the absolute magnitude can be determined in this way then by measuring as well the apparent magnitude, we can determine the distance by the formula: $m - M = 5 \log(d/10)$ where m is the apparent magnitude, M the absolute magnitude and d the distance in parsecs.

Something of a misnomer, this process doesn't really involve parallax at all, but it is a way to get distances. One uses the observed spectrum of the star to obtain the spectral type and luminosity class. These allow you to determine the type of star that it is and to locate it in the HR diagram. From this you obtain the absolute magnitude. The absolute magnitude and the apparent magnitude constitute the distance modulus, from which the distance is obtained.

Spectroscopy : Spectroscopy is the study of the detailed features of a star's spectrum, done by measuring the intensity of the star's light at as many different wavelengths as possible. The resulting spectrum of light allows one to locate the emission and absorption lines, determine the composition of the star, its doppler shift, its spectral type, and its luminosity class.

The study and interpretation of a celestial object's electromagnetic spectrum. A spectrograph or spectrometer is used to analyze an object's electromagnetic spectrum.

Spectrum : A band of colors which forms when visible light passes through a prism. The band ranges in color from violet (shorter wavelength) to red (longer wavelength).

The distribution of wavelengths and frequencies.

Spectrum, Electromagnetic : The distribution of light separated in order of some varying characteristic such as wavelength or frequency. The "electromagnetic spectrum" refers to the full range of possible frequencies and wavelengths of light. If we "take a spectrum" of a star we analyze its light according to wavelength or frequency by, say, passing the light through a prism. A "spectral line" refers to emission or absorption at a particular wavelength of light.

Spectrum, Nonthermal : A continuous spectrum that is not being produced by ordinary thermal processes associated with dense, hot matter (e.g. Blackbody radiation). Synchrotron radiation has a nonthermal spectrum.

Speech Recognition : The use of software to allow computer input of speech; currently only with a restricted vocabulary of words which must be spoken clearly and separately.

Speech Synthesis : The artificial production, by hardware and software through a speaker, of sounds that resemble human speech.

Speed Of Light (c) : The speed at which light (photons) travels through empty space is roughly $3 * 10^8$ meters per second or 300 million meters per second.

= 299,792,458 meters/second (186,000 miles/second). Einstein's Theory of Relativity implies that nothing can go faster than the speed of light; Scotty and Geordi know better.

Spelling Checker : A programme that checks the words of processed text against its list, and takes appropriate action about those it can't find.

Spicules : The grass-like patterns of gas seen in the solar atmosphere.

Spiral Arms : A pinwheel structure, composed of dust, gas, and young stars, that winds its way out from the core of a normal spiral galaxy and from the ends of the bar in a barred spiral galaxy.

Spiral Galaxy : A class of galaxy, spiral galaxies are so named because of their spiral shape.

Galaxy consisting of a flattened rotating disk of stars, a central bulge and a surrounding halo. The disk is prominent due to the presence of young, hot stars which are often arrayed in spiral patterns. The characteristic appearance of these bright spirals gives the galaxy type its name.

A spiral-shaped system of stars, dust, and gas clouds. A typical spiral galaxy has a spherical central bulge of older stars surrounded by a flattened galactic disk that contains a spiral pattern of young, hot stars, as well as interstellar matter.

Spiral galaxy : With the opening of the 100-inch telescope on Mount Wilson near Los Angeles in the early 1920's, astronomers were able to see that there were other galaxies of stars beside our own. These galaxies formed a number of fairly distinct morphological types. The spiral (with a related category of barred spirals) galaxies are the most common. They are distinguished by pinwheel or spiral arms, mixed stellar populations of young and old stars. Regions of star formation, gas and dust. They are classified Sa, Sb, Sc according to increasing prominence of the arms and decreasing prominence of the nucleus.

Spontaneous Bleed : Sudden, unexpected internal bleeding.

Sporadic E : A phenomenon occurring in the E REGION of the IONOSPHERE, which significantly affects HF radiowave Propagation. Sporadic E can occur during daytime or nighttime And it varies markedly with latitude.

Spotnil : Spotless disk

Spreadsheet : A software package that displays a set of entries (such as a firm's accounts) and allows the user to define and redefine the relationships between those entries, showing the effects of any changes automatically.

Sprite : Complex computer graphic units that a user or a programme can control and move as a whole easily. Some games computers have colourful sprites of animals and people built in; others allow users to define or adapt their own.

Sprites : Gamma-ray flashes produced in Earth's atmosphere by severe lightning storms and upper atmospheric events.

S-Process : The absorption of neutrons by elements in massive stars, causing them to transform to other isotopes, and, through subsequent nuclear decay, into other elements. The flux of neutrons is small enough that the process happens slowly (hence "s" process). An important part of the nucleosynthesis of the elements.

Stand-Alone : A system used on its own as opposed to being part of a network, mainframe system or telecommunications link.

Standard : A set of rules and conventions about hardware, software or communications that allows easier links between systems that adopt it.

Standard Candle : A type of object whose brightness is well understood. Standard candles are used to determine how far away distant objects are. Cephied variables and supernovae are used as standard candles.

An object whose properties allow us to measure large distances through space. The absolute brightness of a standard candle can be determined without a measurement of its apparent brightness. Comparing the absolute brightness of a standard candle to its apparent brightness therefore allows us to measure its distance. For example, the distinct variations of Cepheid variable stars in other galaxies tell us their absolute brightness. By accurately measuring the apparent brightness of these stars, astronomers can precisely determine the distance to the galaxy in which they reside. 3. Any astronomical object of known luminosity that can thus be used to obtain a distance. Cepheid variables, Main sequence stars, and type I supernovae have all be used as standard candles.

Standard Time : The time in Greenwich, England, used by scientists by synchronize events. Standard Time is also called Universal Time and Greenwich Mean Time.

Star : A gaseous, self-luminous object held together by its own gravity. The core of a star is extremely hot and releases energy by fusing lighter atomic nuclei into heavier nuclei. Our Sun, the center of our solar system, is a star of average temperature and size.

A network in which each device or node links only to the central switching and control unit.

Star Cluster : A group of stars born at almost the same time and place, capable of remaining together for billions of years because of their mutual gravitational attraction.

Star clusters and associations : Stars normally form in groups. Small groups of 100 stars or less are referred to as associations. Larger groups are the globular clusters containing perhaps half a million stars (Pop. II) which occupy a distribution in space roughly spherical about the centre of the galaxy and extending a long way into the halo, and open or galactic clusters with somewhat fewer stars (Pop. I) normally and which are confined to the galactic plane. Clusters and associations are important in astronomy because they provide samples of stars which are formed at the same time, in the same place, out of the same material. Thus they can be considered to have the same age, distance, and composition.

Starburst Galaxy : A galaxy undergoing an extremely high rate of star formation. Starburst galaxies contain massive, deeply embedded stars that are among the youngest stars observed.

Stefan-Boltzmann Law : This is a law of blackbody radiation that states that the amount of energy given off by a blackbody per second per unit area (see flux) is proportional to the fourth power of the temperature of the blackbody. In practical terms this means that hotter objects give off *a lot* more energy than cooler objects (by the fourth power of the ratio of their temperatures to be exact).

Stefan's law : The energy released by a b-b per unit area per unit time is proportional to the 4th power of the temperature. [We use an expanded form which multiplies this by the surface area for a sphere to give the Luminosity of a b-b as proportional to the square of the radius times the fourth power of the temperature.]

Stellar apparent magnitudes : In the second century B.C.E. Hipparchus devised a system of classifying the stars according to how bright they appeared to the naked eye. He ranked the brightest as magnitude class 1 and the faintest as apparent magnitude 6. All the others were given intermediate values. Because of the logarithmic response of the human eye (similar to that of the ear) we have found that Hipparchus 5 jumps of magnitude correspond to a ratio in luminosity of 100.

Stellar Black Hole : A black hole formed from the death of a massive star during a supernova explosion. A stellar black hole, much like a supermassive black hole, feeds off of nearby material — in this case, the dead star. As it gains mass, its gravitational field increases.

Stellar classification : Stars given a designation consisting of a letter and a number according to the nature of their spectral lines which corresponds roughly to surface temperature. The classes are: O, B, A, F, G, K, and M; O stars are the hottest; M the coolest. The numbers are simply subdivisions of the major classes. The classes are oddly sequenced because they were assigned long ago before we understood their relationship to temperature. O and B stars are rare but very bright; M stars are numerous but dim. The Sun is designated G2.

Stellar Evolution : The process of change that occurs during a star s lifetime from its birth to its death.

Stellar Parallax : The apparent change in the position of a nearby star when observed from Earth due to our planet's yearly orbit around the Sun. This method allows astronomers to calculate distances to stars that are less than 100 parsecs from Earth.

Still Frame : A picture or diagram presented as a single static image rather than as moving footage (compare with freeze frame).

Stishovite : A dense, high-pressure phase of quartz that has so far been identified only in shock-metamorphosed, quartz-bearing rocks from meteorite impact craters.

Stock Control : Describes business software able to handle changing stock levels and reordering needs.

Store : See memory and backing.

Store And Forward : A form of electronic communication in which a message does not go directly to its destination but is stored in a central (host) computer's memory and forwarded later, this being the way many electronic mail systems work.

Stored Programme Concept : A major aspect of the modern computer – it can store the instructions it needs to carry out.

Stored Programme Control (SPC) : Describes (modern digital) telephone exchanges controlled by computer software rather than by permanent wired connections.

Stratosphere : The cold region of a planetary atmosphere above the convecting regions (the troposphere), usually without vertical motions but sometimes exhibiting strong horizontal jet streams.

String : A sequence of any keyboard characters.

Stripe Card : A card (e.g. a credit card) with data held in a stripe so that it can be accessed by a magnetic or optical reader.

Strong Force : The force that binds protons and neutrons within atomic nuclei and is effective only at distances less than 10^{-13} centimeters.

Structure Chart : A diagram that displays the structure of a hardware or software system using boxes on a number of different levels; lower level boxes detail the actions of higher level ones.

Structured Programming : A method of programming whose sections consist of clearly defined and labelled units, each of which one writes, tests, and revises independently.

Subduction : The process of one lithospheric plate descending beneath another.

Sublimation : The change of a solid (such as ice) directly into a gaseous state (bypassing the liquid state). This happens in the vacuum of space with comets, as the heating effects of solar radiation cause ices in comets to "steam off" as gasses into space. The ice molecules present in the nucleus actually break up (or dissociate) into smaller atoms and molecules after leaving the nucleus in gas form.

Sublime : Sublimation occurs when a substance changes directly from a solid to a gas without becoming liquid.

Sudden Commencement (SC, or SSC for Storm Sudden Commencement) : An abrupt Increase or decrease in the northward component of the geomagnetic Field, which marks the beginning of a GEOMAGNETIC STORM.

Sudden Impulse (SI+ or SI-) : sudden perturbation of several gammas In the northward component of the low-latitude geomagnetic field, Not associated with a following geomagnetic storm. (An SI becomes An SC if a storm follows.)

Sudden Ionospheric Disturbance (SID) : HF propagation anomalies due to Ionospheric changes resulting from solar flares, PROTON events And GEOMAGNETIC storms.

Sulcus : Subparallel furrows and ridges.

Sulfuric Acid : A heavy, corrosive, oily, dibasic strong acid H2SO4 that is colorless when pure; it is a vigorous oxidizing and dehydrating agent.

Summer Solstice : The point on the ecliptic where the Sun is farthest north. The summer solstice, which is the longest day of the year, occurs on, or near, June 21, and marks the beginning of summer. See celestial sphere for a helpful diagram.

Sun (Sol) : Big yellow thing visible in the sky during the day, the Sun is by far the largest object in the solar system. It has a mass of 2,000,000,000,000,000,000,000,000,000 kg. It has a diameter of almost 1.4 million km. Over 100,000 Earths could fit inside the Sun! The Sun is composed mostly of hydrogen, and is about five billion years old.

Sunspot : A magnetic storm on the the Sun's surface which appears as a dark area. A sunspot is approximately 1500 degrees Celsius cooler than it's surrounding material. The number of sunspots we see on the Sun at any given time appears to cycle every 11 years.

A region on the Sun's photosphere that is cooler and darker than the surrounding material. Sunspots often appear in pairs or groups with specific magnetic polarities that indicate electromagnetic origins.

Sunspot Cycle : The change in strength of the Sun's magnetic field, which determines the number of sunspots and the amount of particles emitted in the solar wind. The period of the cycle is about 11 years.

Sunspot Group Classification (Modified Zurich Sunspot Classification). A - A small single unipolar SUNSPOT or very small group of Spots without PENUMBRA. B - Bipolar sunspot group with no penumbra. C - An elongated bipolar sunspot group. One sunspot must have Penumbra. D - An elongated bipolar sunspot group with penumbra on both ends Of the group. E - An elongated bipolar sunspot group with penumbra on both Ends. Longitudinal extent of penumbra exceeds 10 deg. But Not 15 deg.F - An elongated bipolar sunspot group with penumbra on both Ends. Longitudinal extent of penumbra exceeds 15 deg. H - A unipolar sunspot group with penumbra.

Sunspot Number : A daily index of SUNSPOT activity (R), defined as R = k (10 g + s) where S = number of individual spots, g = Number of sunspot groups, and k is an observatory factor.

Supercomputer : Loosely applied to the most powerful and fast working types of system.

Superconductivity : The lack of resistance to passing current found in a number of materials at low temperatures.

Superior Planets : The planets Mars, Jupiter, Saturn, Uranus, Neptune and Pluto are called superior planets because their orbits are farther from the Sun than Earth's orbit. (Mercury and Venus are called "inferior" planets.)

Supermassive Black Hole : A black hole possessing as much mass as a million or a billion stars. Supermassive black holes reside in the centers of galaxies and are the engines that power active galactic nuclei and quasars.

Supernova : The explosion of a star. Supernovae come in two types: Type I is caused by sudden nuclear burning in a white dwarf star. Type II is caused by the collapse of the core of a supermassive star at the end of its nuclear-burning life. In either case, the star is destroyed and the light given off in its explosion briefly rivals the total light given off by a whole galaxy.

The explosion resulting when a massive star explodes violently, becoming temporarily brighter than a thousand stars. Because supernovae are so bright, they can be seen from very far away, and thus are useful as standard candles. For more about supernovae, check out the distant supernova search.

Supernova Remnant : The glowing, expanding gaseous remains of a supernova explosion.

The material blown off during a supernova, now seen as a great glowing cloud expanding into space.

Supernova Type I : As discussed above, a white dwarf star, near the 1.4 solar mass limit, can gain mass if it is a companion in a binary system to a star that is going through its giant or supergiant phase. When this happens, the resulting breakdown of degeneracy leads to a supernova explosion in which we believe no stellar remnant is left behind.

Supernova Type II : For stars of initial masses in excess of about 8 solar masses, the successive stages of nuclear fusion lead to the formation of an iron core. Iron is unique in that it requires energy either to fuse it into heavier elements or to fission it into lighter ones. Thus the iron core acts as a sink of energy for the star and triggers an implosion followed almost instantly by an explosion. The result is a supernova type II, causing the ejection of materials at high energies (speeds in excess of 10,000 km/s) producing synchrotron radiation and leaving behind a neutron star remnant. The energy emitted by a supernova can rival that of an entire galaxy for the period of 6 months after the initial explosion during which it gradually declines in brightness.

Supervisor : A type of operating software.

Surge : A jet of material from ACTIVE regions that reaches coronal heights And then either fades or returns into the CHROMOSPHERE along the Trajectory of ascent.

Switched Star : A network layout for cable TV that is specially suitable for interactive services, but tends to be expensive to build.

Switching Centre : A telephone exchange is a switching centre – it switches signals between different lines.

Synchronous Rotation : Said of a satellite if the period of its rotation about its axis is the same as the period of its orbit around its primary. This implies that the satellite always keeps the same hemisphere facing its primary (e.g. The Moon). It also implies that one hemisphere (the leading hemisphere) always faces in the direction of the satellite's motion while the other (trailing) one always faces backward. Most of the satellites in the solar system rotate synchronously.

Synchronous Orbit Radius : The orbital radius at which the satellite's orbital period is equal to the rotational period of the planet. A synchronous satellite with an orbital inclination of zero (same plane as the planet's equator) stays fixed in the sky from the perspective of an observer on the planet's surface (such orbits are commonly used for communications satellites).

Synchronous Rotation : A satellite's rotational period is equal to its orbital period; this causes the same side of a satellite to always face the planet. Synchronous rotation occurs when a planet's gravity produces a tidal bulge in its satellite. The gravitational attraction and bulge acts like a torque, which slows down the satellite until it reaches a synchronous rotation.

Synchrotron (non-thermal) Radiation : First recognized as being produced in particle accelerators, the synchrotron mechanism produces photons as a result of energy being released by high-velocity (relativistic) particles spiralling around the magnetic field lines in a strong magnetic field. While the photons are identical to those produced by Kirchoff's mechanisms (thermal) their spectrum is quite different.

Synchrotron Radiation : Synchrotron radiation is the name for the type of radiation emitted by electrons moving close to the speed of light in the presence of magnetic fields. Two things are required: high speed electrons and magnetic fields. The magnetic force causes the electron (which has a negative electrical charge) to follow a spiral course around the magnetic field. This is an acceleration, and accelerated charges produce electromagnetic radiation. This radiation is produced in pulsars and in active galaxies, and is observed mainly in the radio wavelengths.

Synovial Lining or Membrane : The thin layer of tissue that lines a synovial joint (e.g., knee, ankle, wrist, shoulder). The synovium can become inflamed (synovitis) and sometimes requires surgery to remove part or all of the inflamed membrane (a synovectomy).

Synthesizer : A device for producing artificial speech or music from electronic impulses.

Synthetic-Aperture Radar : SAR is a side-looking imaging system that uses the Doppler effect to sharpen the effective resolution in the cross-track direction.

System : A set of hardware, and maybe software, or a set of working procedures that can carry out a given task.

System X : British Telecom's high speed, high capacity, digital telephone network.

Systems Analysis : A skilled task involving analyzing an information handling need and preparing reports that detail which systems would be suitable for meeting it most efficiently. Systems analysts often have professional programmers working with them.

Systems Software : Software such as the operating system and programming languages that a computer needs to allow it to do anything useful.

❑❑❑

T

Tailor : To modify a hardware system or software package to meet a given user's needs.

Tape : Magnetically or optically coated plastics tape used for holding information – audio, video and computer – accessed by a suitable drive unit.

Target Joint : A joint that has had frequent bleeds; over time, target joints usually develop arthritis.

Target Rocks : The surface rocks that an asteroid or comet impactor smashes into in a meteorite impact event.

TDM : Time division multiplexing.

Teamwork : Working together as a group toward a common goal.

Tectonic : Deformation forces acting on a planet's crust.

Tectonic activity : A shifting of an object's surface due to changes in the material underlying the surface.

Tektites : Natural, silica-rich, homogeneous glasses produced by complete melting, and dispersed as droplets during terrestrial impact events. Tektites range in color from black or dark brown to gray or green and most are spherical in shape. They have been found in four regional deposits or *strewn fields* on the Earth's surface: North America, Czechoslovakia, Ivory Coast and Australasia.

Telebanking : Process of instructing payments and getting account information from a distance, often using viewdata from a terminal in office, shop, or home.

Telecommunications : Transfer and reception of information over a distance.

Telecommuting : Doing one's job from home using IT links to other people's workplaces.

Teleconference : A meeting between people linked by telecommunications, either audio (using telephone lines) or video (using cable).

Telegram : A message sent by telegraph.

Telegraph : Early electric method of transmitting signals using simple on/off codes.

Telescope : An instrument used to observe distant objects by collecting and focusing their electromagnetic radiation. Telescopes are usually designed to collect light in a specific wavelength range. Examples include optical telescopes that observe visible light and radio telescopes that detect radio waves.

Telescopic Observations : Monitoring meteor activity by a telescope, preferably binoculars. This technique is used to determine radiant positions of major and minor showers, to study meteors much fainter than those seen in visual observations.

Teleshopping : Ordering goods at a distance, often using viewdata from a terminal; of value for the busy, elderly, disabled and housebound, as well as in business.

Telesoftware : Software downloaded into a computer's memory over a distance, using telephone lines or broadcast waves.

Teletex : The international standard system for transfer of text and data between terminals using the public telephone network, likely to supersede telex.

Teletext : Information broadcast as part of a television signal, in Britain by Ceefax and Oracle, received on special TV sets with teletext decoders.

Teletype (writer) : A terminal that consists of a keyboard and a printer.

Television (TV) : The transfer of video picture signals, usually with sound, to a screen – either broadcast (mainly by short radio waves) or by cable (mainly in local distribution and closed circuit TV systems).

Telex : A world-wide telegraphic service that allows communication between special printers, by modern standards slow (50 baud), costly and inflexible, but well established and widely available.

Temperature : A measure of the amount of heat energy in a substance, such as air, a star, or the human body. Because heat energy corresponds to motions and vibrations of molecules, temperature provides information about the amount of molecular motion occurring in a substance.

Terminal : Equipment combining input and output hardware to allow the user to communicate with a remote system it may be dumb or intelligent.

Terminator : The dividing line between the illuminated and the unilluminated part of the moon's or a planet's disk.

Terra : An extensive land mass.

Terrestrial : Planets whose density and chemical makeup are similar to those of Earth.

Terrestrial Dynamical Time (TDT or TT) : Time scale used in orbital computations; TDT is tied to atomic clocks (International Atomic Time, TAI), whereas Universal Time is tied to observations. Prior to 1992, Ephemeris Time (ET) was used in publications of the ICQ/CBAT/MPC; since then, TT has been used. The difference between TDT and UTC in 1994 was 60 seconds (i.e., UT + 60 seconds = TDT).

Terrestrial Planets : A type of planet characterized by having a rocky core, and by being small and close to the Sun. Mercury, Venus, Earth and Mars are terrestrial planets.

Tessera : Tile; terrain formed of polygonal pattern

The 21-cm Line of Hydrogen : In 1944, a young Dutch physicist, van de Hulst predicted that hydrogen atoms in the ground state would be able to change their energies by changing from the case where the electron and the nucleus spin in the same direction to a lower state in which they spin in opposite directions. The difference in energy is small and corresponds to a wavelength for an emitted or absorbed photon of 21-cm. Since this radiation comes from hydrogen, the most common constituent of the medium, and since its wavelength is long, and therefore can pass through the interstellar dust easily, this radiation offers a very effective probe of the interstellar hydrogen throughout the galaxy. In fact, under certain assumptions, we can use the 21-cm radiation to map out the distribution of hydrogen throughout the Galaxy.

The Balmer Lines of Hydrogen : Hydrogen has a set of permitted energy levels from the "ground state" (taken as zero energy) to the "ionization limit" (where the electron becomes free). Transitions to or from the 2nd level (or first excited state) are called Balmer lines.

The Bohr Model of The Atom : The atom consists of a positively charged nucleus surrounded by electrons. The electrons move in orbits which are determined by the charge on the nucleus. An atom changes energy only when one (or more) of the electrons change their orbits. Associated with each configuration (distribution of the electron(s) into specific orbits) is an energy. The energy gained or lost is simply the energy of the initial configuration minus the energy of the final configuration. Atoms can change energy via collisions or through the emission or absorption of ONE photon. The wavelength of that photon is inversely proportional to the energy gained (absorption) or lost (emission) by the atom. - the Balmer lines of hydrogen Hydrogen has a set of permitted energy levels from the "ground state" (taken as zero energy) to the "ionization limit" (where the electron becomes free). Transitions to or from the 2nd level (or first excited state) are called Balmer lines.

The Chandrasekhar Limit : In studying the properties of degenerate spheres, Chandrasekhar discovered a strange relationship between the mass and radius of such objects (similar to White Dwarf stars). In particular, rather than increasing with increasing mass, the radius of such an object decreased with mass until, at a mass of about 1.4 solar masses, the radius went to zero. Thus we find no white dwarfs with masses in excess of this value. If we try to increase the mass of a white dwarf beyond this limit, we will trigger a supernova of Type I as the electron degeneracy is "broken through".

The Classification of Stellar Spectra According to Temperature : Because of their different energy levels, different atoms absorb photons at different wavelengths. The "strength" of a specific wavelength depends therefore on two factors: is the element capable of absorbing that wavelength present in the gas (or stellar atmosphere) being studied? If so, are a significant proportion of the atoms of that element in the appropriate energy level to absorb at that wavelength. This in turn is a function of the temperature of the gas. Thus, the absorption spectrum of a star indicates both its composition and its temperature. The current scheme includes the classes (from hottest to coolest) O, B, A, F, G, K, M corresponding to a temperature range from 30,000K to 3,000K.

The CNO Cycle : This is another path by which H is fused to form He. It requires carbon to act as a catalyst and is believed to be the chief mechanism in stars of 3 solar masses and higher which contain carbon.

The Doppler Effect : When a source of light (or sound) is moving towards or away from an observer (radial velocity) the photons (or sound waves) show a shift in wavelength from what would be observed for a stationary source. The ratio of the magnitude of the shift to the rest wavelength is equal to the ratio of the radial velocity to the velocity of light (or sound). The sense of the shift is towards longer wavelengths (redshift) for receding objects and shorter wavelengths for objects coming towards us. This effect is observed in many situations in astronomy and enables us to measure such things as the temperature of stellar atmospheres, stellar atmospheric turbulence, stellar rotation, binary star motions for spectroscopic binaries, individual motions of stars and galaxies relative to the Sun, and the rotation of galaxies.

The Electromagnetic Spectrum : The electromagnetic spectrum covers the total range of possible wavelengths of photons from the shortest "gamma rays" through x-rays, the ultraviolet, the visible, infrared, and microwave to the longest "radio waves".

The Helium Flash : If the He core of a star becomes degenerate in whole or in part (as is the core of the Sun currently) if He fusion is triggered, it starts virtually simultaneously throughout the degenerate region. This is called the "Helium flash". While it is not apparent from outside the star, it does remove the degeneracy of the core by heating the electrons and allowing them more cells in phase space to occupy.

The HR diagram : This is a diagram which plots the Absolute Magnitude of stars vs. Their spectral types. (Alternative forms are luminosity vs. Temperature etc.) Your textbook will have a number of HR (sometimes also called colour-magnitude) diagrams.

The Laws State : First Law: The orbit of a planet is an ellipse with the Sun at one focus. Second Law: The radius vector sweeps over equal areas in equal time intervals. Third Law: The period of a planet squared is proportional to the orbital distance cubed. What this law means is that the further you are from the Sun, the longer it takes to orbit it.

The Lyman Lines of Hydrogen : In this case, the transitions all start or end with the ground state. Whereas the Balmer lines fall in the visible part of the E-M spectrum, the Lyman lines (because of the substantially higher energies involved) fall in the UV part of the spectrum.

The Proton-Proton Chain : While there are a number of processes by which energy may be produced by the fusion of hydrogen into helium, for stars like the Sun the proton-proton chain is the primary mechanism. In it, two protons (hydrogen nuclei) collide to produce a deuterium nucleus. This in turn collides with another proton to form a helium isotope consisting of 2 protons and 1 neutron. Two nuclei of this type them collide to form a normal He nucleus of 2 protons and 2 neutrons while releasing 2 protons. The net effect is thus to convert 4 protons into a He nucleus. During the process, neutrinos and positrons are released as well as photons.

The Red-Giant Branch : As the core contracts and heats in a star that has exhausted its core fuel, the shell source burns more energetically. This causes the outer layers of the star to expand and cool. The star them moves upward and to the right in the HR diagram into the red giant region.

The Russell-Vogt theorem : "The equilibrium structure of a normal star is uniquely dependent on its mass and chemical composition." This principle allows us with confidence to approach the structure of individual stars knowing only their mass and composition.

Thermal Equilibrium : The idea that any energy radiated away from an object (e.g. A star) is replaced by energy generation so that the temperatures remain constant.

A state in which energy is equally distributed among all particles, and all the statistical properties of the particles can be described by a single parameter, the temperature.

At any point in a star, the rate at which energy flows out is equal to the rate at which energy is produced inside that point. Obviously for a point on the surface of a star, the energy outflow (or luminosity) is equal to the rate of energy generation throughout the star.

Thermal Equilibrium : At any point in a star, the rate at which energy flows out is equal to the rate at which energy is produced inside that point. Obviously for a point on the surface of a star, the energy outflow (or luminosity) is equal to the rate of energy generation throughout the star.

Thermal Line : A known radio emission line.

Thermal Pulse : A sudden increase in temperature caused by a dramatic increase in a nuclear burning rate. Although it falls short of what we would call an explosion, it does drive a dynamic readjustment in the star.

Thermal Radiation : Radiation released by virtue of an object's heat, namely, the transfer of heat energy into the radiative energy of electromagnetic waves. Examples of thermal radiation are sunlight, the orange glow of an electric range, and the light from in incandescent light bulb.

Thermometer : An instrument for measuring temperature.

Thimble : The printhead of a type of printer; its shape is much like that of a thimble, and its outside carries raised characters. The thimble turns and nods to bring each character into contact with the paper.

Tholus : A small domical mountain or hill.

Thomson, William 1824-1907 : Aka Lord Kelvin, British physicist who developed the Kelvin scale of temperature. Also supervised the laying of a trans-Atlantic cable. (10k gif)

Tidal Forces : The gravitational pull on planetary objects from nearby planets and moons. When the tidal forces of a planet and several moons are focused on certain moons, particularly if the orbits of the various objects bring them into alignment on a repeated basis, the tidal forces can generate a tremendous amount of energy within the moon. The intense volcanic acivity of Io is the result of the interaction of such tidal forces.

Tidal Heating : Frictional heating of a satellite's interior due to flexure caused by the gravitational pull of its parent planet and possibly neighboring satellites.

Tight Beam : Describes signals sent by radio (for instance) to a single destination.

Time Division Multiplexing (TDM) : A method of sending several messages down a single communications channel by giving each source a time slot in turn.

Time of Perihelion Passage : The time at which an object is at perihelion (it's closest distance to the sun).

Time Sharing : A method of allowing a processor to work on several jobs at once, by sharing its time between them.

To find out what the Universal time is click here. Warning! This can be slow!

Tombaugh, Clyde 1906-1997 : American astronomer; discovered Pluto.

Topocentric : Refers to a reference system centered at some location on the Earth (for example, the geographic location of an observatory). The topocentric distance to an object is the distance between the object and the topocenter (for example, the observer).

Total (visual) Magnitude : Total, integrated magnitude of a comet's head (meaning coma + nuclear condensation). This can be estimated visually, as the comet's "total visual magnitude". The variable m_1, usually found in comet ephemerides, is used to denote the total (often predicted) magnitude. See also definition for "Magnitude", above.

Touch Screen : A touch sensitive screen allowing the user to make choices by pointing with a finger, thus making the screen act as an input device as well as displaying output. Some touch screens detect pressure; others sense the interruption of a criss-cross grid of infra-red beams. Used in computer and interactive video systems aimed at the general public, and anywhere the traditional keyboard may present a barrier.

Tracker Ball : A computer input device consisting of a ball set in a socket; as you turn the ball with the palm of your hand a pointer moves over the screen. The tracker ball is much like a mouse or joystick in its effect.

Tracking and Data Relay Satellite System (TDRSS) : A network of four communication satellites used to relay data and commands to and from U.S. spacecraft, including the Hubble Space Telescope. The Goddard Space Flight Center provides the day-to-day management and operations of TDRSS, the first space-based global tracking system.

Trailing Hemisphere : The hemisphere that faces backwards, away from the direction of motion of a satellite that keeps the same face toward the planet.

Trajectory : The line of motion of the meteor relative to the Earth, considered in three dimensions.

Transborder Data Flow : The transfer of information (as text, broadcast signals or data) across national borders.

Transportable : More accurate adjective for microcomputers that are too big and heavy to be truly portable; also used to describe software that will run on different computers to some extent.

Transputer : A very powerful 32-bit processor on a chip with a RAM store that can be linked to others to provide parallel processing.

Tree : A method of arranging data, viewdata pages, or cable TV networks that resembles the trunk, branches, and twigs of a tree.

Trekkie : (also "Trekker") a devotee of the science fiction program Star Trek.

Trigonometric Parallax : The trigonometric parallax of an object is the angle (in seconds of arc, 1/3600 of a degree) subtended at that object by a baseline of length 1 astronomical unit (A.U., approximately 150-million kilometers). This is the basis for virtually all forms of distance determination in astronomy. The parsec is a unit of distance which corresponds to a parallax of one second of arc. It is equivalent to 206,265 A.U. or 3.26 light years. It is inversely proportional to the parallax.

Triple Alpha Reaction : The process by which helium (also known as an alpha particle) is converted into carbon. When temperatures are high and the density of helium is large, three helium atoms can combine to form one Carbon atom. Hence the name: 3 helium reaction.

Triton : The largest of Neptune's satellites. Triton has an atmosphere and is roughly the size of Earth's moon. It has an "ice cap" of frozen nitrogen and methane with "ice volcanoes" that erupt liquid nitrogen, dust, and methane compounds from beneath its frozen surface.

Trojan Satellites : Satellites which orbit at the Lagrangian points, 60° ahead of and 60° behind another satellite. For example, Telesto and Calypso are trojans of Saturn's satellite Tethys.

Troposphere : The lower regions of a planetary atmosphere where convection keeps the gas mixed and maintains a steady increase of temperature with depth. Most clouds are in the troposphere.

T-Tauri Star : A class of very young, flaring stars on the verge of becoming normal stars fueled by nuclear fusion.

Ttrigonometric Parallax : The trigonometric parallax of an object is the angle (in seconds of arc, 1/3600 of a degree) subtended at that object by a baseline of length 1 astronomical unit (A.U., approximately 150-million kilometers). This is the basis for virtually all forms of distance determination in astronomy. The parsec is a unit of distance which corresponds to a parallax of one second of arc. It is equivalent to 206,265 A.U. or 3.26 light years. It is inversely proportional to the parallax.

Tuff : The general term for consolidated pyroclastic debris.

Tully-Fisher Relation : An empirical relationship between the width of the 21-cm line of hydrogen emissions from spiral galaxies, and the mass of the galaxy. The relationship arises because a larger mass increases the rotation rate, and a faster rotation causes a broader line; the precise calibration must be determined observationally.

Turbulence : Unstable and disorderly motion, as when a smooth, flowing stream becomes a churning rapid.

Turnkey System : A computer system supplied in a complete and customized form so that the user need only 'turn the key' to start it.

TV/Monitor : A display that can either display TV pictures or act as a monitor. Some can do both jobs at once and show computer text and graphics on top of a video picture.

TWO-RIBBON FLARE : A FLARE that has developed as a pair of bright strands (ribbons) on both sides of the main inversion ("neutral") line Of the magnetic field of the ACTIVE REGION.

TYPE I, II, III, IV : See RADIO EMISSION

Typesetter : An advanced form of word processing system that lets one prepare fully edited and laid-out pages of text and perhaps graphics for printing; also called desktop publisher.

❏❏❏

U

U BURST. A fast radio burst spectrum of a FLARE. It has a U-shaped appear- Ance in an intensity-vs.-frequency plot.

UHF : Ultra high frequency; usually applied to electromagnetic waves.

ULA : Uncommitted logic array: a type of chip which contains circuits not yet connected. Its manufacturer can add different final layers containing the interconnections to suit different purchaser's requirements. The result is much cheaper than making a fully customized chip.

ULSI : Ultra large scale integration: a method of packing a very large number (more than 1,000,000) of electronic components and their connections on to a single chip (compare with LSI and VLSI).

Ultra High Frequency (UHF) : Those radio frequencies exceeding 300 mhz.

Ultraviolet Rays : Invisible electromagnetic radiation which is comprised of very short wavelengths. Human beings get a sunburn from the ultraviolet rays emitted by the Sun.

Ultraviolet (UV) **:** Electromagnetic radiation with shorter wavelengths and higher energies and frequencies than visible light. UV light is lower in frequency than X-rays.

Umbra : The dark core or cores (umbrae) in a SUNSPOT with PENUMBRA, or a Sunspot lacking penumbra.

Universal Precautions : Actions taken during exposure to people's blood and other body fluids to prevent the transmission of infectious diseases; involves the use of protective procedures and equipment, such as disposable gloves.

Universal time (UT) : See COORDINATED UNIVERSAL TIME.

Universal Time (UT, or UTC) : A measure of time used by astronomers; UT conforms (within a close approximation) to the mean daily (apparent) motion of the sun. UT is determined from observations of the diurnal (daily) motions of the stars for an observer on the earth. UT is usually used for astronomical observations, while Terrestrial Dynamical Time (TDT, or simply TT) is used in orbital and ephemeris computations that involve geocentric computations. Coordinated Universal Time (UTC) is that used for broadcast time signals (available via shortwave radio, for example), and it is within a second of UT.

Universe : The totality of space and time, along with all the matter and energy in it. Current theories assert that the universe is expanding and that all its matter and energy was created during the Big Bang.

Universe : The vast expanse of space which contains all of the matter and energy in existence.

UNIX : A popular and sophisticated operating system for 16-bit microcomputers that allows multi-users and multi-tasking.

Unsettled : With regard to geomagnetic levels, a descriptive word speci- Fically meaning that 8 is less than or equal to the Ap INDEX which is less than or equal to15.

Upgrade : The process of improving or adding to hardware or software. A good system will have a well planned upgrade path, so that software can be transferred on to expanded hardware without wasted effort.

Upper Case : Describes capital letters.

Upstream : Messages sent by cable system users towards the centre are said to go upstream. The transmission speed needed for upstream messages depends on their nature.

Uranus : The seventh planet from the Sun, Uranus is a gas giant planet with at least seventeen moons. It is also well known because of its peculiar axis of rotation, which is almost parallel to the ecliptic. Check out SEDS' Nine Planets, for more about Uranus. Or see stardate's Solar System Guide. Uranus.

The third largest planet in the solar system and the seventh from the Sun. Uranus is 19 times the Earth's distance from the Sun and completes a circuit around the Sun in about 84 Earth years. This gaseous, giant outer planet has a visible ring system and over 20 moons, the largest of which is Titania. Uranus is tipped on its side, with a rotation axis in nearly the same plane as its orbit.

User Friendly : Describes IT systems believed by their designers to be easy to use. In practice many turn out to be user hostile.

User Interface : Front end, or man-machine interface – the mode of interaction between a system and a user and its associated hardware and software.

Utilities : Programmes that allow users to do useful jobs like copying discs or recovering deleted files.

❐❐❐

V

Vallis : A sinuous valley.

VAN : Value added network: one that provides subscription services like electronic mail and viewdata in addition to basic telecommunications facilities.

Van Allen Belt : A region containing charged particles trapped in the Earth's magnetic force field (magnetosphere). The belt's lower boundary begins at about 800 kilometers (496 miles) above the Earth's surface and extends thousands of kilometers into space.

Van Allen, James A. : American physicist who discovered the Earth's radiation belts (that now bear his name) with an instrument aboard the first successful American satellite, Explorer 1.

Variable Star : A star whose luminosity (brightness) changes with time.

At various periods in the evolution of a star, it may enter a phase in which some of its properties (luminosity, temperature, radius, magnetic field, etc.) May vary in a more or less regular way. Such stars are called variables. They are important because the specific form of the variability is associated with a specific region in the HR diagram. In addition, the period of variability may be related to the inherent brightness of the star. Thus the Cepheid variables are important indicators of distance because of the relation between their period and brightness and because they are supergiants that can be seen at great distances (even nearby galaxies).

Vasoconstriction : The narrowing of a blood vessel to shrink a wound and reduce blood flow; occurs when a cold compress or ice is applied to the skin.

Vastitas : Widespread lowlanas.

VCR : Video cassette recorder.

VDU : Visual display unit.

Vela Satellite : Launched by the U.S. in the 1960s to monitor the Limited Nuclear Test Ban Treaty. The satellite's mission was to detect the gamma rays produced during nuclear blasts. Although not intended for astronomical studies, the Vela satellite provided useful celestial data, detecting an unexpected blast of cosmic gamma radiation in 1967. The satellite discovered several other gamma-rays bursts during the years of the Vela project, which ceased operation in 1979.

Velocity : The speed of an object moving in a specific direction. A car traveling at 35 miles per hour is a measurement of speed. Observing that a car is traveling 35 miles per hour due north is a measurement of velocity.

Venipuncture : Insertion of a needle into a vein to infuse replacement factor.

Vent : The opening in the crust through which volcanic material erupts.

Venus : An inner, terrestrial (rocky) planet that is slightly smaller than Earth. Located between the orbits of Mercury and Earth, Venus has a very thick atmosphere that is covered by a layer of clouds that produce a "greenhouse effect" on the planet. Venus's surface temperature is roughly 480° C (900° F), making it the hottest planet in the solar system.

Venus has an orbit of 108 million km. It is the second planet from the Sun. Venus is very similar to Earth in many ways: both have roughly the same diameter and mass, both are terrestrial Planets and both have the same chemical make-up.

Verification : The process of checking computer input or action for certain types of mistake. To verify means to check whether saving a file, formatting a disc, or entering data to a system was successful.

Vernal Equinox : The point on the celestial sphere where the Sun crosses the Earth's equatorial plane from south to north. Also called the first point of Aries.

The place in the sky where the Sun crosses the celestial equator moving northwards. The vernal equinox falls on, or near, March 21, the first day of spring. See celestial sphere for a helpful diagram.

The point on the celestial sphere where the sun crosses the celestial equator moving northward, which corresponds to the beginning of spring in the northern hemisphere and the beginning of autumn in the southern hemisphere (in the third week of March). This point corresponds to zero (0) hours of right ascension.

Verne, Jules 1828-1905 **:** French writer who is considered the founder of modern science fiction. His novels include "Journey to the Center of the Earth" and "From the Earth to the Moon".

Vertical Markets : Software designed for a particular client group (e.g. solicitors or cocoa factories) rather than to perform a particular function (e.g. spreadsheet or word processing).

Very High Frequency (VHF) : That portion of the radio frequency spectrum From 30 to 300 mhz.

Very Large Array (VLA) **:** One of the world's premier radio observatories, consisting of 27 antennas arranged in a huge "Y" pattern. The VLA spans up to 22 miles (36 km) across, which is roughly one and a half times the size of Washington, D.C. Each antenna is 81 feet (25 meters) in diameter. Located in Socorro, New Mexico, the telescopes work in tandem to produce a sharper image than any single telescope could record.

Very Low Frequency (VLF) : That portion of the radio frequency spectrum from 3 to 30 khz.

VHD : Video high density: a form of video disc.

VHF : Very high frequency: usually referring to electromagnetic waves used for TV.

Video : Describes hardware and systems working with VHF signals.

Video Camera : A device whose electronic output represents the scene that it scans.

Video Cassette : Cassette containing video tape.

Video Cassette Recorder (VCR) : A machine that records and plays back video tape packed in cassettes.

Video Disc : A plastics, metal, or glass disc that can store large numbers of moving or still video pictures with sound. Unlike video cassettes, data can be quickly accessed at random on some video discs. As they can also store digital information, this gives them great potential as a medium for computer memory because of their enormous capacity. At present, however, video discs cannot generally be recorded on to by the user.

Video Phone : A telephone which can transmit an image from a camera and put one received on to a screen, as well as handling speech in the normal way.

Video Tape : High density magnetic tape on which video pictures and sound can be recorded.

Videoconference : A 'meeting' between people in different places using video links for the transfer of speech, data and pictures.

Videotex : Electronic methods of receiving certain types of information from a distance and displaying it on a screen; may use broadcasting signals (teletext) or telephone lines (viewdata). Teletext is often referred to as one-way or broadcast videotex, and viewdata as two-way or interactive videotex. Videotext is an alternative spelling sometimes used in the US.

Viewdata : A two-way transfer of electronic information using telephone lines and TV sets. Local users cannot only retrieve information from large databases but also send messages and instructions. Prestel was the world's first public viewdata system.

Visible Light : Electromagnetic radiation that human eyes can detect; also known as the visible spectrum. The visible colors are red, orange, yellow, green, blue, indigo, and violet, along with various combinations and shades of these colors. Within the visible part of the spectrum, red light has a longer wavelength than blue light.

Visual Binary : A binary star system that can be resolved into separate stars in direct observations. In binary systems that are not visual, the two stars are so close that they can't be distinguished (resolved) in observations.

Visual Display Unit (VDU) : A device that displays computer output on a screen; also used loosely to mean a combined screen and keyboard unit.

Vlsi : Very large scale integration: a method of packing a very large number (1000 to 1,000,000) of electronic components and their connections on to a single chip (see also LSI and ULSI).

Vmos : An acronym for Very Massive Object, vmos are dark matter candidates which are thought to be 100 times more massive than our Sun. They are likely to be found in the form of black holes.

Voice Bank : A public telephone answering service.

Voice Grade : Describes a communication channel suitable for the transfer of speech.

Voice Mail : See digital voice messaging.

Voice Recognition Unit : A computer input device that can be 'trained' to identify spoken words.

Voice Response Systems (VRS) : Users can telephone messages, orders and questions to these computer-based information systems. The computer responds immediately in a high quality synthesized voice, delivering information or confirmation in the appropriate language.

Voice Traffics : The use of a telephone system to carry conversations as opposed to data.

Volatile : As a noun, this refers to substances that are gases at ordinary temperatures. In astronomy it includes hydrogen, helium, water, ammonia, carbon dioxide and methane.

Volatile : Describes computer memory whose contents are lost when you switch off.

Volcanism : Volcanic activity.

Volcano : (1) A vent in the planetary surface through which magma and associated gases and ash erupt. (2) The form or structure produced by the erupted materials. (3) A break or vent in the crust of a planet or moon that can spew extremely hot ash, scorching gases, and molten rock. The term volcano also refers to the mountain formed by volcanic material.

Von Willebrand Disease (vwd) : A bleeding disorder in which platelets do not gather properly when blood vessels are injured, resulting in incomplete formation of platelet plugs and mucosal bleeding. The most common bleeding disorder, von Willebrand disease occurs equally in males and females.

VRS : Voice response systems.

❒❒❒

W

WAN : Wide area network.

Wand : Light pen.

Wave : A vibration in some media that transfers energy from one place to another. Sound waves are vibrations passing in air. Light waves are vibrations in electromagnetic fields.

Wavelength : A wave is an oscillation in space, with peaks and troughs. The distance from one peak to the next is the wavelength. It is measured in units of distance. The wavelength of ocean water waves will be meters. The wavelengths of visible light corresponds to hundreds of nanometers (billionths of a meter). Wavelength is an important way to characterize a wave. For light, the shorter the wavelength, the higher the energy of the light wave.

Wavelength : The distance between two peaks (or troughs) on a wave; the larger the wavelength, the lower the frequency.

Weak Force : The force that governs the change of one kind of elementary particle into another. This force is associated with radioactive processes that involve neutrons.

Weight : The gravitational force exerted on a body.

White Dwarf : A whitish star of high surface temperature and low intrinsic brightness with a mass approximately equal to that of a Sun but with a density many times larger.

The remnant of a star, at the end of its life, consisting of a carbon and oxygen core supported by electron degeneracy pressure. The surface has a very high temperature and radiates mainly in the ultraviolet (hence white as in white hot), but it is only about the size of the Earth (hence dwarf). The maximum mass that can be supported by electron degeneracy pressure, and hence the maximum possible mass of a white dwarf, is known as the Chandrasekhar mass and is equal to 1.4 solar masses.

The hot, compact remains of a low-mass star like our Sun that has exhausted its sources of fuel for thermonuclear fusion. White dwarf stars are generally about the size of the Earth.

White Light (WL) : Sunlight integrated over the visible portion of the spec- Trum (4000 - 7000 angstroms) so that all colors are blended to Appear white to the eye.

White Light Flare : A major FLARE in which small parts become visible in White light. Such flares are usually strong X-ray, radio, and Particle emitters.

Wide Area Network (WAN) : A method for linking computers and terminals that are widely separated, often using public or private telephone lines. Transmission speeds may be lower than in a LAN, but WANs often span immense distances.

Wide Field / Planetary Camera (WF/PC) **:** A collection of eight separate, yet interconnected, cameras originally used as the main optical instrument on the Hubble Space Telescope. Four cameras were used in tandem to observe in either wide-field, low-resolution mode or narrow-field, high-resolution ("planetary") mode. The Wide Field and Planetary Camera 2 replaced the WF/PC during the December 1993 servicing mission.

Wide Field and Planetary Camera 2 (WFPC2) **:** The Hubble Space Telescope's "workhorse" instrument, WFPC2 snaps high-resolution images of faraway objects. Its 48 filters allow scientists to study precise wavelengths of light and to sense a range of wavelengths from ultraviolet to near-infrared light. The instrument has four ccds (charge-coupled devices), which collect information from stars and galaxies to make photographs. WFPC2 was installed aboard the Hubble telescope during the December 1993 servicing mission.

Wideband : Same as broadband – describing a communications channel with a large bandwidth, at least 10 kilobaud.

Wien's Law : The wavelength at which the b-b spectrum reaches peak intensity is inversely proportional to the temperature.

This is the law of light that says for blackbody emission, the higher the temperature of the blackbody emitter, the higher the frequency (or shorter the wavelength) of the predominant light it emits. The specific relation is (Peak Wavelength) = 0.29/T where the wavelength is given in centimeters and T in degrees Kelvin.

Wimp : An acronym for a Weakly-Interacting Massive Particle. A particle with a nonzero mass which participates only in the weak nuclear interaction. Such particles (currently hypothetical) could fill space and provide gravitational force without any associated luminosity. As such they are a candidate for dark matter.

An exotic class of non-baryonic particle, wimps (Weakly Interacting Massive Particles) are a prime dark matter candidate. For more about dark matter and wimps, check out these pages: The question of dark matter The WIMP experiment Big bang cosmology primer

Wimp : Windows, icons, mouse and pointers (or pull-down menus): describes a modern, flexible and friendly type of user interface.

Winchester : A type of sealed hard disc unit very popular for use with micro-computers. Originally 350 mm in diameter, Winchesters have become progressively smaller, yet give ever greater capacities and faster access time.

Windows : The effect of splitting a display screen into two or more separate sections, each able to hold different types of data to be interacted with and processed separately.

Winter Solstice : The point on the ecliptic where the Sun is farthest south. The winter solstice, which is the shortest day of the year, occurs on, or near, December 21, and marks the first day of winter. See celestial sphere for a helpful diagram.

Wired Society : A catchphrase to suggest the social implications of improved modern communications.

Wolf Number : An historic term for SUNSPOT NUMBER. In 1849, R. Wolf of Zurich originated the general procedure for computing the sunspot Number.

WOOD : Write once optical disc.

Word : Processors do not deal with individual bits of information; they group them into uniform 'words' and process each as a single unit. Many older personal computers have a word length of eight bits, newer machines work on 16-bit or even 32-bit words.

Word Processing (WP) : A system for editing, storing and rearranging text so that it can be perfected before being finally printed out Word processed text can be produced easily and without errors to give (for instance) 'personalized' letters containing variations on a standard text. Any computer can word process if it has suitable software and peripherals.

Word Processor : Strictly, a machine dedicated to word processing, but loosely used to describe any computer that is running word processing software.

Worksheet : A database or file set up in the form of a spreadsheet, with a row for each record and a column for each field.

Workstation : The place where an individual user interacts with an IT system; loosely, a terminal.

WORM : Write once, read many times: describes a type of optical disc.

WP : Word processing.

Write : To write to a disc, for instance, is to copy data to it for storage (compare with read).

Write Once Optical Disc (WOOD) : A type of video disc on which the user can record, but from which information cannot be erased.

WYSIWYG : What you see is what you get: describes a word processing system whose display of text is somewhat like a printout would be.

❑❑❑

X

X Chromosome : The sex chromosome that is paired (XX) in female cells and single (XY) in male cells.

X25 : An international standard protocol for packet switching.

Xerography : The technique behind modern photocopiers and some page printers which charges a drum electrostatically in the pattern of the original material, the charge attracting a plastics dust (toner) which then bakes on to the paper.

X-Linked : A gene that is transmitted by the X chromosome. Hemophilia is an X-linked, recessive trait.

X-Ray : A class of high energy photon, X-rays have wavelengths of 0.012 to 12 nanometers. Not only are X-rays used for medical imaging (when you break your arm an X-ray machine is used to take a picture of the broken bone), but since black holes, quasars, and other stellar objects emit X-rays, X-Ray Astronomy is actively researched.

Electromagnetic radiation of very short wavelength and very high energy; x-rays have shorter wavelengths than ultraviolet light but longer wavelengths than cosmic rays.

X-Ray Astronomy : A branch of astronomy which deals primarily with X-Rays.

X-Ray Background : A daily average background X-ray flux in the 1 to 8 Angstrom range. It is a midday minimum designed to reduce the Effects of flares.

X-Ray Burst : A temporary enhancement of the X-ray emission of the sun. The Time-intensity profile of soft X-ray bursts is similar to that of The H-ALPHA profile of an associated FLARE.

X-Ray Burster : A semidetached binary system where matter is accreting onto a neutron star. As hydrogen accretes onto a neutron star (possibly producing a variable X-ray source) the hydrogen is promptly burned into helium. The helium accumulates until the temperature is high enough for a degenerate helium burning explosion.

X-Ray Flare Class : Rank of a FLARE based on its X-ray energy output. Flares Are classified by the order of magnitude of the peak burst inten- Sity (I) measured at the earth in the 1 to 8 angstrom band as Follows: Class (in Watt/sq. Meter) B I less than (l.t.) 10.0E-06 C 10.0E-06 l.e.= I l.t.= 10.0E-05 M 10.0E-05 l.e.= I l.t.= 10.0E-04 X I g.e.= 10.0E-04

❑❑❑

Y

Year : The period required for an object to orbit a star once. Note that the length of a year depends upon where you are: an Earth year is 365 days, but a Pluto year is almost 250 Earth *years*.

Young : When used to describe a planetary **surface** "young" means that the visible features are of relatively recent origin, i.e. That older features have been destroyed (e.g. By erosion or lava flows). Young surfaces exhibit few impact craters and are typically varied and complex. In contrast an "old" surface is one that has changed relatively little over geologic time. The surfaces of Earth and Io are young; the surfaces of Mercury and Callisto are old.

❒❒❒

Z

Zenith : The point directly overhead in the sky. The scientific method The scientific method has evolved as the most reliable approach to the development of models to explain natural phenomena. Basically it provides a cycle in which theories to explain natural phenomena are tested against further observations. To be successful, a theory must meet this test and, hopefully, provide an explanation of a broader range of observations than those on which it was based. If not, it is either refined or discarded and the cycle begins again. Astronomy, unlike astrology, follows the scientific method and is therefore classified as a science.

Zero Age Main Sequence (ZAMS) : The theoretical line of the main sequence which corresponds to the onset of hydrogen burning and the beginning (zero age) of a star's life.

Zero Lnhibitor : The absence of an inhibitor.

Zodiacal Light : A faint glow from light scattered off of interplanetary dust along the plane of the ecliptic.

Zurich Sunspot Classification : A sunspot classification system that has been Modified for SESC use.

❑❑❑